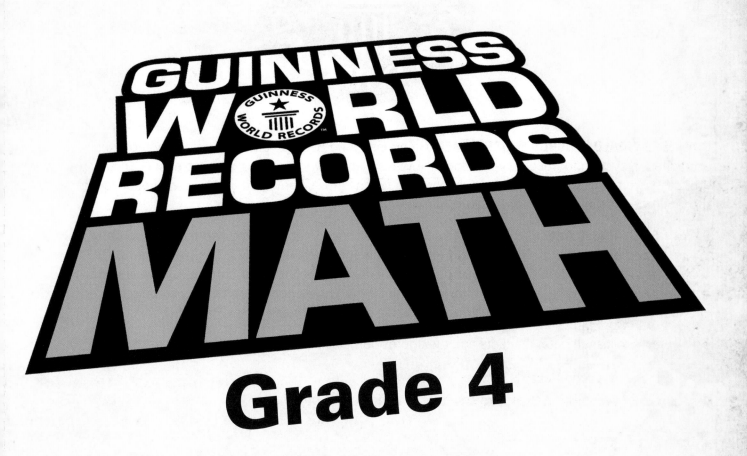

Grade 4

by Nancy Rogers Bosse

Carson-Dellosa Publishing LLC
Greensboro, North Carolina

Credits

Content Editors: Elizabeth Swenson and Amy R. Gamble
Copy Editor: Julie B. Killian
Layout and Cover Design: Van Harris

This book has been correlated to state, common core state, national, and Canadian provincial standards. Visit *www.carsondellosa.com* to search for and view its correlations to your standards.

Carson-Dellosa Publishing LLC
PO Box 35665
Greensboro, NC 27425 USA
www.carsondellosa.com

ISBN 978-1-936024-03-2
03-079121151

Introduction 4
Skills Matrix 8

Amazing Animals
An Eye for Color 10
One Big "Hoppy" Family 12
That Baby Can Eat! 14
Built for Speed 16
Let Her Roll! 18
An Amazing Migration 20
Whoa—That's a Tall Horse! 22
Easy-to-Find Eyelashes 24
Those Are Some *Baa-d* Horns! 26
A Supersize Snail 28
My, What Big Teeth You Have! 30
Little Dog, Big Job 32
What Is Heavy and Has Eight Legs? 34

Earth Extremes
Growing Wild 36
Now, That's Spelunking! 38
What a Watermelon! 40
How Hot Is Hot? 42
This Geode Rocks! 44
This Will Blow You Away! 46
Glow-in-the-Dark Bacteria? 48
Johnny Appleseed Would Be Proud! 50
Martian Meteorite Mystery 52
Giant Waves from Nowhere 54

Wild, Wacky & Weird
A Lot Longer Than a Foot Long 56
Long May She Wave 58
How Would You Like Your Eggs? 60
Great Gobs of Green Goo! 62
Superheroes Set Super Record 64
On Top of the World 66
Texting One, Two, Three 68
Not Your $5 Pizza 70

For a Pink Cause 72
An Amazing Maze 74
Coins for a Cause 76

Engineering, Science & the Body
Pedal Power 78
A Mighty Grand Dam 80
Powered by the Sun 82
Ready for Takeoff! 84
A Hod-Headed Man 86
A Nail-Biting Record—Not! 88
Sending the Very Tallest 90
More Than Most 92
A Real Spider Man 94
A Treasure Trove 96
A Large Lady of Liberty 98
Share the Power 100

Game Time!
This Will Make Your Head Spin! 102
At a Loss for Words? 104
Jumping Jacks in a Flash 106
Gnarly Dude! 108
Chain Reaction 110
B-I-N-G-O! 112
Out of Gas? 114
Go Team! 116
Around the World 118
Hey, Batter Batter! 120
Ping, Pong, and Repeat 122
The Karate Master 124

Answer Key 126

INTRODUCTION

A man held the tails of 11 rattlesnakes in his mouth. Eight elephants painted a picture that sold for $39,000. A tailor sewed a pair of underpants that measured 40 feet from the waistband to the crotch. The largest stick insect is 22 inches long. Welcome to the wild, wacky, and amazing achievements of Guinness World Records™!

Guinness World Records is the authority on feats that are of interest to the world or have historic importance. Since the first publication of *The Guinness Book of Records* in 1955, readers have laughed, gasped, and gagged at the details. Students are especially drawn to the facts. Short, exciting, and to the point, the records open up a fascinating world to explore, in both human endeavors and nature's endless marvels.

It is a natural step to pair students' interests in world records with math. To be a record, the achievement has to have qualities that can be measured (weight, height, distance, speed, or monetary value, for example) and compared (lightest, tallest, slowest, etc.). The numbers provide endless opportunities to practice math skills and strategies in a fun way. Wow, that dog broke the record by jumping three inches higher! The biggest spider could fill my dinner plate! I like roller coasters, so riding one for 405 consecutive hours would be fun. But, wait! That's nearly 17 days!

MAKING GUINNESS WORLD RECORDS™

Guinness World Records accomplishments are facts that belong in one of eight categories:

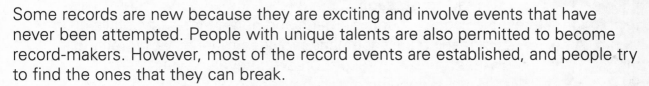

- Human Body
- Amazing Feats
- Natural World
- Science and Technology
- Arts and Media
- Modern Technology
- Travel and Transport
- Sports and Games

Some records are new because they are exciting and involve events that have never been attempted. People with unique talents are also permitted to become record-makers. However, most of the record events are established, and people try to find the ones that they can break.

Guinness World Records receives more than 60,000 requests per year. Record-makers and breakers must apply first so that their attempts are official. The organization sets guidelines for each event to make sure that it can be properly measured. Guinness World Records also makes sure that record-breakers follow the same steps so that each participant gets an equal chance. Professional judges make sure that the guidelines are followed correctly and measured accurately. However, the guidelines may designate other community members who can serve as judges to witness an event. Once the record attempt is approved, the participant gets a framed certificate. The person's name may also be included in the yearly publication or on the Guinness World Records Web site at *www.guinnessworldrecords.com*.

World Record Themes

Guinness World Records™ *Math* is divided into five themes, each focusing on 10 to 14 exciting records:

- Amazing Animals
- Earth Extremes
- Wild, Wacky & Weird
- Engineering, Science & the Body
- Game Time!

Math Passages

Each left page features a reading passage about a remarkable world record. This engaging, high-interest passage recounts numeric and human-interest details of the record. A box on each reading passage page provides more amazing records relating to the featured record-maker or record-breaker. Leveled writing ensures success for all students. An eye-popping color photograph of the accomplishment accompanies each passage to support the content.

Math Word Problems

On each right page, five to six word problems focus students' attention on the details of the records, allowing students to practice math skills in a real-world application. Formats include fill-in-the-blank, multiple choice, matching comparisons, and tables, graphs, and charts. Problems increase in difficulty and include a variety of math strands and cognitive levels. Nearly every page provides practice in critical thinking skills and mixed measurement conversions.

BE A RECORD-BREAKER!

Hey, kids!

At age 10, Tiana Walton put 27 gloves on her hand. Mark Aldridge was 17 when he popped 56 balloons with the end of his pogo stick in one minute. Eighty-five-year-old Saul Moss went scuba diving in the ocean. So, why are these people important? They are Guinness World Records™ record-makers and record-breakers! Walton, Aldridge, and Moss did something truly amazing!

A world record is a weird, wacky, or amazing achievement that is a fact. It can be a skill someone has, such as popping the most balloons with a pogo stick, or it can be an interesting part of nature, such as the smelliest bird. Guinness World Records has judges who set rules to make sure that all record-makers and record-breakers follow the same steps. Then, the judges count, weigh, measure, and compare to make sure that the achievement is the greatest in the world.

So, can you be a Guinness World Records record-breaker? If you can run, hop, toss, or even race with an egg on a spoon, you just might see your name on a record. With the help of an adult, visit *www.guinnessworldrecords.com*. There you will find a world of exciting records to explore— and maybe break!

 The Carson-Dellosa Team

SKILLS MATRIX

Page Number	Whole Numbers	Fractions and Decimals	Operations	Money and Time	Algebra	Measurement	Data Analysis
11	✔	✔	✔	✔	✔		✔
13	✔	✔	✔		✔	✔	
15	✔	✔	✔	✔	✔	✔	
17	✔	✔	✔	✔		✔	
19	✔	✔	✔	✔	✔	✔	✔
21	✔		✔	✔		✔	
23	✔	✔	✔			✔	
25	✔	✔	✔	✔		✔	
27	✔	✔	✔			✔	
29	✔	✔	✔	✔		✔	
31	✔	✔	✔	✔		✔	✔
33	✔	✔	✔	✔		✔	
35	✔	✔	✔			✔	✔
37	✔	✔	✔	✔	✔	✔	
39	✔	✔	✔			✔	✔
41	✔	✔	✔		✔	✔	
43	✔	✔	✔		✔	✔	✔
45	✔	✔	✔		✔	✔	
47	✔	✔	✔	✔	✔	✔	
49	✔	✔	✔			✔	
51	✔		✔	✔			✔
53	✔	✔	✔	✔		✔	✔
55	✔	✔	✔			✔	✔
57	✔	✔	✔	✔	✔	✔	
59	✔		✔	✔			
61	✔	✔	✔	✔			✔
63	✔	✔	✔	✔		✔	
65	✔		✔	✔		✔	
67	✔		✔			✔	
69	✔	✔	✔	✔			✔

Page Number	Whole Numbers	Fractions and Decimals	Operations	Money and Time	Algebra	Measurement	Data Analysis
71	✔	✔	✔	✔			
73	✔		✔			✔	
75	✔	✔	✔		✔	✔	
77	✔	✔	✔	✔			
79	✔		✔	✔	✔	✔	
81	✔	✔	✔			✔	✔
83	✔	✔	✔	✔		✔	
85	✔	✔	✔	✔		✔	
87	✔	✔	✔		✔	✔	
89	✔	✔	✔	✔	✔	✔	✔
91	✔		✔	✔	✔	✔	✔
93	✔	✔	✔	✔		✔	✔
95	✔		✔	✔	✔		
97	✔		✔	✔		✔	
99	✔		✔			✔	
101	✔	✔	✔	✔		✔	✔
103	✔		✔	✔	✔	✔	✔
105	✔	✔	✔		✔	✔	
107	✔		✔	✔			
109	✔	✔	✔			✔	
111	✔		✔	✔	✔		✔
113	✔		✔	✔	✔	✔	✔
115	✔	✔	✔	✔		✔	
117	✔	✔	✔	✔	✔		
119	✔	✔	✔	✔	✔		✔
121	✔	✔	✔	✔		✔	
123	✔		✔	✔		✔	
125	✔	✔	✔	✔	✔	✔	

AN EYE FOR COLOR

■ Check this out!
Greatest Color Vision

The mantis shrimp is so strong that it can shatter the glass of a fish tank! But, the mantis shrimp has other powerful body parts—its eyes. The mantis shrimp holds the Guinness World Records™ record for the Greatest Color Vision. Its eyes have 8 receptors, or color-sensing parts of the eyes. These receptors can sense colors that are invisible to other animals.

Humans' eyes have 3 receptors that can see about 10,000 colors. Dogs' eyes only have 2 receptors, and they cannot see some colors that humans can. With its 8 color-sensing receptors, the mantis shrimp sees 10 times more colors than we do!

MORE AMAZING RECORDS

Hottest Fish Eyes: The world's Hottest Fish Eyes belong to the swordfish. It can heat its eyeballs to as much as 82°F. This helps the swordfish see prey up to 12 times faster than it could with cold eyes.

Largest Eyes: The world's Largest Eyes belonged to an Atlantic giant squid found in 1878. The record-setting eyeballs measured 15.75 inches in diameter.

First Artificial Eye: The use of the world's First Artificial Eye was announced in January 2000. Made up of a camera, distance sensor, and computers, the device helped a man see for the first time in 36 years!

Name_____ Date_____

■ Answer the questions. Show your work.

1. In what **year** did the man who received the First Artificial Eye lose his sight?

2. Round the diameter of 1 of the Atlantic squid's eyes to a whole number.

3. **About** how many colors can the mantis shrimp see? Write an equation to show your thinking.

4. _____ have 1/4 **fewer** color receptors than the mantis shrimp.

5. Which Celsius temperature is equal to the temperature that the swordfish can heat its eyes to?
    A. 0°C
    B. 28°C
    C. 82°C
    D. 100°C

6. Draw a **table** to show the data in the main passage. Give the table a title.

ONE BIG "HOPPY" FAMILY

■ Check this out!

Longest Rabbit

The rabbits in this family keep hopping into the record books. The world's Longest Rabbit is the daughter of the former record-holder. Alice is a continental giant rabbit. She is 3 feet 3 inches long.

Amy, Alice's mother, held the previous record. Amy was 2 feet 8 inches long. Now, Alice's son Darius is trying for the record. At 4 feet 3 inches, he is still growing!

This furry family is owned by Annette Edwards (UK). She got her first rabbit when she was 8 years old. Certainly, Edwards is raising one big "hoppy" family!

MORE AMAZING RECORDS

Longest Lizard: The slender Salvadori, or Papuan monitor lizard, is the world's Longest Lizard. It is 15 feet 7 inches long. Almost 70 percent of its length is its tail.

Longest Insect: The *Phobaeticus serratipes* stick insect is the world's Longest Insect. It is 21 inches long, including its legs. Its body length is 11 inches.

Name_____ Date_____

■ Answer the questions. Show your work.

1. Number the record-setting animals in order from **shortest** to **longest**.

   _____ rabbit   _____ lizard   _____ insect

2. Alice is 3 feet 3 inches long. Write Alice's length in feet as a mixed number.

3. How much longer is Darius the rabbit than the world's Longest Insect?

4. If the world's Longest Lizard's tail measures 130.9 inches, how long is the lizard's body in inches?

5. Which equation shows how much longer Alice is than Amy in **inches**?
   A. (12 x 3 + 3) – (12 x 2 + 8) = 7 inches
   B. 3.3 – 2.8 = 0.5 inches
   C. (3 – 2) + (8 – 3) = 6 inches
   D. (12 x 3) – (2 x 12) + (3 + 8) = 23 inches

6. **Estimate** how many times longer the Longest Lizard is than Alice the rabbit. Explain your thinking. Check your estimate.

THAT BABY CAN EAT!

■ Check this out!

Greediest Animal

Babies need food to grow. But, the larva of the polyphemus moth set the world record for being the Greediest Animal. In its first 56 days, this larva eats 86,000 times its birth weight. Most babies eat about 2.5 ounces times their weight per day. Just imagine—that would be the same as a 7-pound human baby eating 273 tons of food!

The larva is inside an egg that is about 0.1 inches long. The first meal the larva eats is its own eggshell. The larva grows to about 3 inches.

This greedy eater changes into one of the biggest moths. Unlike the larva, adult polyphemus moths do not eat. In fact, they do not even have mouths!

MORE AMAZING RECORDS

Longest Time a Bird Has Gone Without Food: A record-setting male emperor penguin did not eat for 134 days! It is common for male emperor penguins to stop eating during a part of mating season. These birds are able to survive because of the fat stored in their bodies. This fat can be about 1.2 to 1.6 inches thick. During the time of not eating, these birds lose more than 1/2 of their body weight.

Hungriest Bear Species: The giant panda is the world's Hungriest Bear Species. To survive, giant pandas must eat as much as 38 percent of their own weight in bamboo shoots or as much as 15 percent of their own weight in bamboo leaves and stems—every day!

Name_____ Date_____

■ Answer the questions. Show your work.

1. The larva of the polyphemus moth eats 86,000 times its weight at birth in

   the first _____ weeks of life.

2. How many **inches** does the polyphemus moth grow from egg to
   full-grown larva before it makes a cocoon?

3. The male emperor penguin went without food for **about** _____ months.

4. If the larva of the polyphemus moth eats the same amount each day, **about**
   how many times its birth weight does it eat in 1 day? Round the answer to the
   nearest hundred.

5. Which equation shows the **average** thickness of the emperor penguin's fat?
   - **A.** 1.6 − 1.2 = 0.4 inches
   - **B.** 1.6 + 1.2 = 2.8 inches
   - **C.** (1.6 + 1.2) ÷ 2 = 1.4 inches
   - **D.** (1.6 − 1.2) x 2 = 0.8 inches

6. **About** how many times her weight would a 7-pound human baby eat in
   56 days if she stayed the same weight?

BUILT FOR SPEED

■ Check this out!

Fastest Mammal on Land over Short Distances

In the wild, cheetahs can maintain a speed of 62 miles per hour for a short distance. They are built for speed! On February 24, 1999, a cheetah named Nyana set the Guinness World Records™ record for world's Fastest Mammal on Land over Short Distances. He ran 328 feet in 6.19 seconds. Nyana averaged about 36.8 miles per hour. He reached a top speed of 68.4 miles per hour. His stride length was 24 feet, and he took about 2 strides per second.

Nyana is owned by Annie Beckhelling (South Africa). Beckhelling started the Cheetah Outreach program, which teaches people about cheetahs and raises money to help protect them.

MORE AMAZING RECORDS

Fastest Mammal on Land over Long Distances: Pronghorns are animals similar to antelopes and deer. They can travel at speeds of 35 miles per hour for as far as 4 miles. Their strides can reach 26 feet!

Fastest Primate: Patas monkeys are the world's Fastest Primates. They can reach speeds of 34 miles per hour.

© Carson-Dellosa

■ Answer the questions. Show your work.

1. Nyana could travel **about** _____ feet in 1 second.

2. **About** how many strides did Nyana take to travel 328 feet? Round the answer to the nearest whole number.

3. Write the speeds of Nyana the cheetah, the pronghorn, and the patas monkey on the number line.

$$\xleftarrow{\quad}\overset{\displaystyle|}{33}\quad\overset{\displaystyle|}{34}\quad\overset{\displaystyle|}{35}\quad\overset{\displaystyle|}{36}\quad\overset{\displaystyle|}{37}\xrightarrow{\quad}$$

4. Draw a line from each distance traveled to the time it would take Nyana to travel that distance. Estimate using 328 feet in 6.19 seconds as the reference.

3,936 inches	about 3 seconds
327 yards	about 18 seconds
1,640 feet	6.19 seconds
164 feet	about 30 seconds

5. How many strides would a pronghorn take over a distance of 4 miles? Round the answer to the nearest whole number.

6. **Estimate** how many strides Nyana would take if he ran at his **average** speed for 1/2 hour?

LET HER ROLL!

■ Check this out!
Fastest Caterpillar

When you think of record speeds, you probably do not think of a caterpillar. But, the larva of the mother-of-pearl moth set the record for being the Fastest Caterpillar in the world. It can travel 15 inches in 1 second! That is a rate of almost 0.9 miles per hour.

This type of caterpillar is able to move so quickly by rolling itself into a ball. Only a handful of creatures can curl up and roll away if attacked. This caterpillar's speed helps it survive.

At about 0.7 inches long, the caterpillar's body is made up of 13 parts, and its legs connect to each of those parts. The caterpillars walk at about 0.39 inches per second. No wonder they know how to roll!

MORE AMAZING RECORDS
Fastest Chelonian: *Chelonian* is a group of reptiles that includes turtles. The highest speed for any chelonian in water is 22 miles per hour, set by a Pacific leatherback turtle.

Fastest Crocodile on Land: The world's Fastest Crocodile on Land is the freshwater crocodile. This Australian species can reach a speed of 10.56 miles per hour.

Name_____ Date_____

■ Answer the questions. Show your work.

1. Which **fraction** represents the rolling speed of a mother-of-pearl moth larva?

   A. $\frac{9}{100}$ of a mile per hour   B. $\frac{9}{10}$ of a mile per hour

   C. $\frac{9}{60}$ of a mile per hour   D. $\frac{9}{1}$ miles per hour

2. One complete roll of the Fastest Caterpillar is 360°. Draw a line from each degree to the **equivalent fraction** of a roll.

   90° $\frac{1}{2}$ of a roll

   180° $\frac{3}{4}$ of a roll

   270° $\frac{1}{4}$ of a roll

3. Write the length of 1 of the caterpillar's parts as a fraction.

4. How much **faster** does the caterpillar roll than walk per second?

5. **About** how many times faster is the Pacific leatherback turtle than the crocodile?

6. Draw a table to show how many inches the caterpillar rolls in 1 second, 10 seconds, 30 seconds, and 1 minute. Write a **rule** to show how to calculate the values in the right-hand column.

AN AMAZING MIGRATION

■ Check this out!
Longest Fish Migration

Did you know that fish migrate? One Pacific bluefin tuna set the world record for the Longest Fish Migration. It traveled about twice the distance of the United States, but in the ocean!

So, how is a migration like this recorded? First, a research team catches the fish. Then, they weigh, tag, and release the fish. When the fish reaches its new location, the team retags it.

The record-setting fish was first tagged off the coast of Mexico in 1958. It was retagged just south of Japan in 1963. It had traveled a distance of about 5,800 miles! During its journey, the tuna's weight increased from 35 pounds to 267 pounds. That does not leave a lot of time for sightseeing!

MORE AMAZING RECORDS

Longest Insect Migration: One male monarch butterfly traveled at least 2,880 miles.

Longest Mammal Migration: The humpback whale migrates up to 5,095 miles each way.

Longest Bird Migration: The Arctic tern is a small bird similar to a seagull. This species of bird migrates 21,750 miles round trip!

Longest Land Animal Migration: Grant's caribou travels up to 2,982 miles each year.

Name_____ Date_____

■ Answer the questions. Show your work.

1. How much weight did the Pacific bluefin tuna gain on its record-setting trip?

   A. 132 pounds

   B. 232 pounds

   C. 302 pounds

   D. 267 pounds

2. How many years passed between when the tuna was tagged off the coast of Mexico and when it was tagged just south of Japan?

3. Order the tuna, butterfly, whale, tern, and caribou by their **one-way** migration distances from shortest to longest.

4. The Arctic tern migrates **about** _____ times farther than the humpback whale.

5. Suppose a 10-foot-long Pacific bluefin tuna weighs 1,200 pounds. If its weight were even all over its body, how much would it weigh per foot? Explain your thinking.

6. If the Pacific bluefin tuna traveled at a rate of 15 miles per hour, **about** how many days would it take it to travel 5,800 miles without stopping? Explain your thinking.

WHOA—THAT'S A TALL HORSE!

■ Check this out!

Tallest Horse Living

Many people know that a horse is a tall animal. But, this Belgian gelding raises the standard even higher. On January 19, 2010, he set the Guinness World Records™ record for the world's Tallest Horse Living.

Big Jake measured 20 *hands* 2.75 inches high without shoes. Big Jake was measured 3 times with the same measurement recorded each time. He is owned by Smokey Hollow Farms in Poynette, Wisconsin.

Horses and mules are measured in units called *hands*. One hand is equal to 4 inches. A horse is measured from the ground to the highest point of its withers (shoulders). Most horses are about 16 hands high.

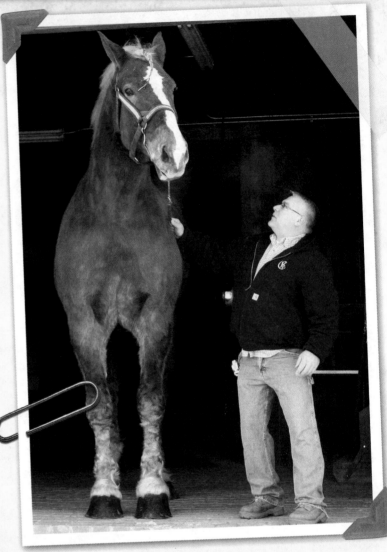

MORE AMAZING RECORDS

Tallest Mule: Apollo is the world's Tallest Mule. His height was recorded at 19 hands.

Tallest Mammal: The word's Tallest Mammal is the giraffe. The tallest giraffe ever recorded stood 19 feet. His name was George.

Tallest Ox: Fiorino, the world's Tallest Ox, measured 6 feet 8 inches tall.

Name_____ Date_____

■ Answer the questions. Show your work.

1. How many hands equal 1 foot?

2. In inches, how much taller is Big Jake than most horses?

3. About how tall is Big Jake in feet and inches?

    A. 5 feet 10 inches

    B. 6 feet 10 inches

    C. 7 feet 6 inches

    D. 6 feet 2 inches

4. Is Big Jake **taller** than the world's Tallest Ox? Explain your thinking.

5. If a giraffe were measured in **hands**, how many hands tall would the tallest giraffe be?

6. Order the record-setting animals from shortest to tallest. On another sheet of paper, draw a picture showing the **relative heights** of each animal.

    _____ horse   _____ mule   _____ giraffe   _____ ox

EASY-TO-FIND EYELASHES

■ Check this out!

Longest Eyelashes on a Dog

Have you ever gotten an eyelash in your eye? If this record-holder got one in his eye, he could have a real problem. One of his eyelashes is 5.35 inches long! A dog named Prince Albert set the record for having the world's Longest Eyelashes on a Dog.

Prince Albert is a breed of dog called a Lhasa Apso. These dogs stand about 10 inches tall. They are known for their mop-like coats.

Prince Albert, owned by Sandra Daku of Canada, has held this record since November 27, 2004. At least if Prince Albert gets an eyelash in his eye, it would not be hard to find!

MORE AMAZING RECORDS

Most Expensive Dog: A Tibetan mastiff named Yangtze River Number Two sold for $563,000.00!

First Dog Film Star: Rollie Rover starred in the film *Rescued by Rover* in 1907.

Most Dogs Walked at the Same Time by 1 Person: Melissa Crispin Piche (Canada) holds the record for walking 27 dogs at the same time!

Name_____ Date_____

■ Answer the questions. Show your work.

1. Which tool would be the best for measuring the height of Prince Albert?
   - **A.** 12-inch ruler
   - **B.** yardstick
   - **C.** 50-foot tape measure
   - **D.** scale

2. Rollie Rover set the record for being the world's First Dog Film Star more than a _____ ago.
   - **A.** decade
   - **B.** century
   - **C.** half century
   - **D.** millennium

3. For the record-setting eyelash to be 5.5 inches long, it would have to grow _____ inches. Write the answer as a decimal.

4. If someone with $1 million bought Yangtze River Number Two, how much money would he **have left**?

5. Suppose you walked 27 dogs, each valued at the same price as the world's Most Expensive Dog. How much would the dogs be worth **altogether**?

6. The record-setting eyelash was on Prince Albert's left eye. The longest eyelash on his right eye was 5 inches long. **About** what fraction of an inch longer was his longest left eyelash than his longest right eyelash?

THOSE ARE SOME *BAA-D* HORNS!

■ Check this out!

Longest Domestic Goat Horns

These record-setting horns are long—really long. A goat named Uncle Sam set the Guinness World Records™ record for the Longest Domestic Goat Horns. His horns spanned 52 inches from tip to tip!

Uncle Sam's horns were so long that they had a slight curl. His left horn measured 39.33 inches, and his right horn measured 40.12 inches. Uncle Sam's record-setting horns were measured on April 16, 2004.

Uncle Sam was owned by Bill and Vivian Wentling. They own a farm in Rothsville, Pennsylvania. Now, Pennsylvania has one more historic American symbol to call its own!

MORE AMAZING RECORDS

Longest Sheep Horn: The longest horn found on a species of sheep measured 75 inches. The horn belonged to a Marco Polo sheep in the Pamir Mountains.

Longest Bull Horns: The world's Longest Bull Horns each measured 4 feet 7 inches. They belonged to a bull named Gopal.

Longest Horns: The world's Longest Horns of any living animal are those of the Asian water buffalo. The horns of one bull measured 13 feet 10 inches from tip to tip.

Name_____ Date_____

■ Answer the questions. Show your work.

1. If you measured Uncle Sam's horns along the curls, what would be the total length of both horns?

2. How much longer is the horn span from tip to tip of the Asian water buffalo than the horn span of Uncle Sam?

3. Write the length in feet of the world's Longest Bull Horns as a mixed number.

4. **About** how many times longer are the Longest Sheep Horns than the Longest Domestic Goat Horns?

5. What is the difference in feet and inches between Uncle Sam's horn span and someone who is 6 feet tall?

A SUPERSIZE SNAIL

■ Check this out!

Largest Snail

You might expect a snail to set the record for the slowest animal in the world. But, this snail set the record for being the world's Largest Snail. Named Gee Geronimo, this supersize snail was owned by Christopher Hudson (UK). It measured 15.5 inches from snout to tail. It weighed a whopping 2 pounds! It has held the record since December 1978.

Gee Geronimo was an African giant snail. Although this type of snail looks like the common garden snail, the African giant snail is much bigger. The shell of most garden snails is only about 1.18 inches long. But, the shell of an African giant snail can measure up to 10.75 inches long!

MORE AMAZING RECORDS

Fastest Racing Snail: The world's Fastest Racing Snail is named Archie. He sprinted a 13-inch course in exactly 2 minutes.

Most Snails on the Face: The most snails kept on the face for 10 seconds is 48. This record was set by Mike Dalton (Australia).

Fastest Land Snail: The Fastest Land Snail is the garden snail. A garden snail named Verne completed a 12.2-inch course in 2 minutes, 13 seconds.

28

Name_____ Date_____

■ Answer the questions. Show your work.

1. As of January 1, 2010, how many years had Gee Geronimo held the record for the world's Largest Snail?

2. What is the **difference** in length between the shell of an average garden snail and the shell of an average African giant snail?
   - A. 9.93 inches
   - B. 11.93 inches
   - C. 9.63 inches
   - D. 9.57 inches

3. How much **longer** was the track that Archie raced on than the track that Verne raced on?

4. Which snail is **faster**—Archie or Verne? Explain your thinking.

5. If the line below represents the length of the world's Largest Snail from snout to tail, show how much of the line would be its shell. How much would be left as its head and tail? Round all of the decimals to the nearest whole number.

_____

6. **Estimate** the weight of a garden snail. Explain your thinking.

MY, WHAT BIG TEETH YOU HAVE!

■ Check this out!
Largest Teeth Compared to Head Size for a Fish

Creatures that live deep in the ocean often look very unusual. The Sloan's viperfish is no exception. It holds the Guinness World Records™ record for Largest Teeth Compared to Head Size for a Fish. The viperfish's body is about 11 inches long. Its head measures about 0.8 inches. But, its teeth measure about 0.5 inches each! This means that the viperfish's teeth are more than 1/2 the length of its head!

Viperfish migrate up and down in the ocean. During the day, they live about 8,000 feet below the surface. At night, they swim up to a depth of about 2,000 feet because it is easier to find food in shallower water. With teeth like the viperfish, aren't you glad you are not their prey?

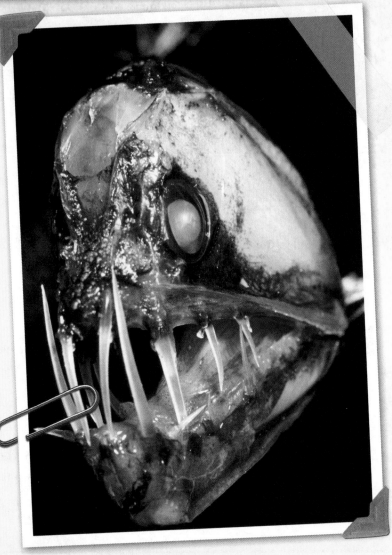

MORE AMAZING RECORDS

Longest Whale Tooth: The world's Longest Whale Tooth is that of the male narwhal. His teeth average about 6 feet 6 inches long. Some may grow as long as 9 feet 10 inches.

Land Mammal with the Most Teeth: The giant armadillo is the Land Mammal with the Most Teeth. This mammal typically has 100 teeth.

Dinosaur with the Most Teeth: The duck-billed *Hadrosaurus* was the dinosaur with the most teeth. It is believed to have had 960 teeth!

Name_____ Date_____

■ Answer the questions. Show your work.

1. A Sloan's viperfish is **about** the length of _____ .
    - **A.** a sheet of paper
    - **B.** a large paper clip
    - **C.** your hand
    - **D.** your desk

2. What is the **range** of the average and the longest male narwhal's tooth?

3. How far does the Sloan's viperfish migrate in 24 hours?

4. What is the **difference** in length between a viperfish's teeth and the tooth of an average male narwhal?

5. Suppose you lined up 100 viperfish teeth. How long would they measure in all?
    - **A.** 0.5 inches
    - **B.** 50 inches
    - **C.** 5 inches
    - **D.** 500 inches

6. **Estimate** how long 1 of your teeth would be if it were about 1/2 the size of your head.

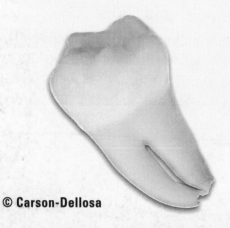

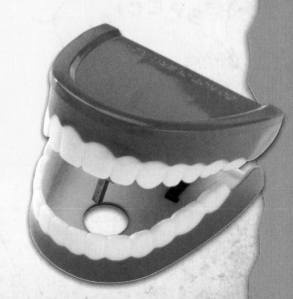

LITTLE DOG, BIG JOB

■ Check this out!
Smallest Police Dog

When you think of police dogs, you may think of German shepherds. But, the world's Smallest Police Dog is a cross between a Chihuahua and rat terrier. Her name is Midge, and she is only 11 inches tall and 23 inches long. That includes her 7-inch tail!

Midge may not look like a police dog, but she is an official K9. She is trained to sniff out drugs. She is small enough to search in cars and school lockers.

Midge lives and works with her owner, Sheriff Dan McClelland, in Chardon, Ohio. Midge was born on November 6, 2005. She passed the police dog test just 1 year later. Midge may not be a big dog, but she has a big job!

MORE AMAZING RECORDS

Most Successful Sniffer Dog: Snag, a Labrador retriever, has made 118 drug recoveries with a total cost of $810,000,000.00!

Most Successful Police Dog: The world's Most Successful Police Dog is a golden retriever named Trepp. He has been credited with more than 100 arrests and the recovery of drugs worth $63,000,000.00.

Most Guide Dogs Trained: The Guide Dogs for the Blind Association in the United Kingdom broke the record for Most Guide Dogs Trained. As of 2006, the association had successfully trained 26,019 dogs to help blind or partially sighted people.

Name_____ Date_____

■ Answer the questions. Show your work.

1. How old will Midge be in 2020?

2. Midge's tail is **about** what fraction of the length of her body?

A. $\frac{1}{2}$ of her body   **B.** $\frac{1}{3}$ of her body

C. $\frac{1}{4}$ of her body   **D.** $\frac{3}{4}$ of her body

3. How many **more** dogs would the Guide Dogs for the Blind Association need to train to reach 1 million dogs?

4. What is the **difference** between the cost of drugs recovered by Snag and Trepp? Write the difference in word form.

5. If Snag and Trepp are both 22 1/2 inches tall, how much taller than Midge are they?

6. Using a ruler, draw a picture of Midge to scale. Use the scale 1/16 of an inch equals 1 inch.

WHAT IS HEAVY AND HAS EIGHT LEGS?

■ Check this out!
Heaviest Spider

What is heavy, has 8 legs, and is about the size of a dinner plate? Rosi! Rosi is the world's Heaviest Spider. In July 2007, she weighed in at a whopping 6.17 ounces!

Rosi is a female Goliath bird-eating spider. These big spiders do not usually eat birds though. They eat insects, frogs, lizards, snakes, and small rodents. Goliath bird-eating spiders can grow to more than 11 inches long!

Goliath bird-eating spiders have fangs that are about 1 inch long. The spiders also rub their legs together to make a hissing sound. This sound can be heard from 15 feet away. So the next time a spider is in your garden, be glad it is not a Goliath bird-eating spider!

MORE AMAZING RECORDS

Heaviest Bird of Prey: The world's Heaviest Bird of Prey is the Andean condor. It can weigh up to 27 pounds and has a wingspan of about 10 feet.

Heaviest Scorpion: The world's Heaviest Scorpion is the large emperor scorpion. It can weigh up to 2 ounces. It measures between 5 and 7 inches long.

Heaviest Poisonous Snake: The eastern diamondback rattlesnake is the world's Heaviest Poisonous Snake. It weighs between 12 and 15 pounds and is about 5 to 6 feet long. The heaviest diamondback rattlesnake on record weighed 34 pounds and was 7 feet 9 inches long.

Name_____ Date_____

■ Answer the questions. Show your work.

1. The hissing sound that the Goliath bird-eating spider makes can be heard

   from _____ **yards** away.

2. Is the Goliath bird-eating spider more than or less than **twice** the
   length of the world's Heaviest Scorpion? Explain your thinking.

3. Rosi's weight in ounces is closest to which weight **in pounds**?

   A. 1 pound

   B. $\frac{3}{4}$ of a pound

   C. $\frac{1}{2}$ of a pound

   D. $\frac{1}{4}$ of a pound

4. Up to how much can the Andean condor weigh in **ounces**?

5. The line below represents ounces. Place a dot to show **about** where 6.17 ounces
   would be located.

6. If you calculate the average weight of an eastern diamondback rattlesnake, will your results
   represent the **typical** weight of a diamondback rattlesnake
   if you include the weight of the **heaviest** diamondback
   rattlesnake in your data? Explain your thinking.

GROWING WILD

■ Check this out!

Fastest-Growing Flowering Plant

If you have ever grown flowers in your garden, you know that it can take some patience. But if you lack patience, you may want to grow a yucca! The yucca holds the Guinness World Records™ record for the Fastest-Growing Flowering Plant. It can grow 11 feet 11 inches in just 14 days. That is about 10 inches per day!

This record was reported by people from Tresco Abbey, Isles of Scilly. The plant also grows wild in southern California and parts of Arizona. Because this plant grows wild, it is probably better viewed on a hike than in your garden!

MORE AMAZING RECORDS

Fastest-Growing Plant: The world's Fastest-Growing Plant is bamboo. It can grow up to 35 inches per day! The tallest reported bamboo plant was 130 feet tall. In the United States, bamboo typically grows to between 65 and 98 feet tall!

Fastest-Growing Marine Plant: The giant kelp is the world's Fastest-Growing Marine Plant. It grows about 13.3 inches per day.

Fastest-Growing Individual Tree: The record-setting tree was planted on June 17, 1974, in Sabah, Malaysia. The tree grew 35 feet 2.8 inches in 13 months. That is about 1.1 inch per day!

Name_____ Date_____

■ Answer the questions. Show your work.

1. Which record-breaker grows **closest** to 1 foot per day?
   - **A.** yucca
   - **B.** bamboo
   - **C.** kelp
   - **D.** tree

2. If the yucca were to keep growing at the same rate, how tall would it be in 20 days? Write the answer in feet and inches.

3. **About** how many days did it take the tallest reported bamboo plant to reach 130 feet tall?

4. Draw a line from each plant to how much it could grow in **30 days**.

   yucca   300 inches

   bamboo   399 inches

   kelp   1,050 inches

   tree   33 inches

5. Write an **equation** to determine how tall the tallest reported bamboo plant is in inches. Solve the equation.

6. **Estimate** how long it would take for the giant kelp to reach 10 feet long. Explain your thinking.

NOW, THAT'S SPELUNKING!

■ Check this out!

Largest Cave

Are you a spelunker? A spelunker is someone who explores caves. The world's Largest Cave is the Sarawak Chamber. It is 2,300 feet long. Its average width is about 980 feet. It is at least 230 feet high. That is big enough to hold about 38 football fields!

Carlsbad Caverns is the largest cave in the United States. It was once the largest known cave. But, the Sarawak Chamber is 3 times larger than Carlsbad Caverns.

MORE AMAZING RECORDS

Largest Land Gorge: The Grand Canyon in the United States is more than 277 miles long! In some places, it reaches up to 1 mile deep. Its width is between 0.25 to 18 miles, with an average width of 10 miles.

Largest Slot Canyon: The Narrows in Zion National Park, Utah, is almost 2,000 feet deep. Its walls are only 30 feet apart at their widest points. The canyon is 16 miles long!

The Sarawak Chamber is part of the Lubang Nasib Bagus cave. This cave is in the Gunung Mulu National Park in Sarawak, Malaysia. This national park is as big as Singapore, a country in Asia. Imagine spelunking a cave this size!

Name_____ Date_____

■ Answer the questions. Show your work.

1. What is the **range** of the width of the Grand Canyon?

2. Which of the following could **not** be a width measurement of the Grand Canyon?
  - **A.** 16 kilometers
  - **B.** 16,000 meters
  - **C.** 1,600,000 centimeters
  - **D.** 16 kilograms

3. The Sarawak Chamber is about _____ **yards** long. Round the answer to the nearest whole number.

4. Estimate the area of the Sarawak Chamber.

5. Estimate the area of Carlsbad Caverns. Explain your thinking.

6. How could you measure the length of the Sarawak Chamber using 25 feet of measuring tape? Explain your thinking.

WHAT A WATERMELON!

■ Check this out!

Heaviest Watermelon

Ever enjoy a slice of watermelon on a hot day? Well, the world's Heaviest Watermelon could feed a lot of people on a hot day. In 2005, the record-breaking melon weighed in at 268.8 pounds!

Lloyd Bright of Arkadelphia, Arkansas, grew this enormous melon. It was not his first watermelon record either. He broke his first record in 1979. That melon weighed 200 pounds.

So, just how amazing is this record? An average serving size of watermelon is 2 cups per person. Bright's record-setting melon could feed more than 435 people!

MORE AMAZING RECORDS

Heaviest Mango: The world's Heaviest Mango weighed 7.57 pounds. It measured 12 inches long. Its circumference measured 19.5 inches.

Heaviest Cauliflower: The world's Heaviest Cauliflower weighed 54 pounds 3 ounces.

Heaviest Carrot: The world's Heaviest Carrot weighed 18 pounds 13 ounces. The top of the carrot measured 11.75 inches around.

Heaviest Tomato: The world's Heaviest Tomato weighed 7 pounds 12 ounces.

Name_____ Date_____

■ Answer the questions. Show your work.

1. Which of the following weighs **about the same** as the record-breaking watermelon?

   A. a small dog

   B. a dump truck

   C. a baseball bat

   D. a large trash can filled with garbage

2. How could you calculate the weight of the world's Heaviest Watermelon in ounces? Explain your answer.

3. Draw a line from each record-breaking garden food to its weight in ounces.

   watermelon   301 ounces

   mango   867 ounces

   cauliflower   124 ounces

   carrot   4,300.8 ounces

   tomato   121.12 ounces

4. **About** how many record-setting mangoes would you need to equal the weight of the world's Heaviest Watermelon? Explain your thinking.

5. Write an equation to determine the **diameter** of the world's Heaviest Mango. Assume that the mango is a perfect circle around the middle.

6. How could you find the **diameter** of the world's Heaviest Carrot using a ruler?

HOW HOT IS HOT?

■ Check this out!

Highest Recorded Temperature

"It is hot enough to fry an egg!" This saying is often used to describe a really hot day. The day with the world's Highest Recorded Temperature was definitely hot enough to fry an egg. It was 136°F—and that was in the shade!

This Guinness World Records™ record was set in the Sahara Desert on September 13, 1922. The Sahara Desert is in northern Africa. It covers more than 3,500,000 square miles. It is the largest desert in the world. Some sand dunes are over 390 feet high!

Death Valley, California, set the record for the second-highest temperature. It was 134°F, which is definitely hot enough to fry an egg!

MORE AMAZING RECORDS

Lowest Temperature: The world's Lowest Temperature ever recorded was in Vostok, Antarctica. It was -128.6°F on July 21, 1983.

Greatest Temperature Range in 1 Day: The world's Greatest Temperature Range in 1 Day happened in Browning, Montana. The temperature dropped from 44°F to -56°F!

Greatest Temperature Ranges on Earth: The Greatest Temperature Ranges on Earth happen around the Siberian "cold pole" in the eastern part of Russia. Temperatures in Verkhoyansk have ranged from -90°F to 98°F.

Name_____ Date_____

■ Answer the questions. Show your work.

1. An average football field is 100 yards long. Compare the length of a football field to the height of a sand dune in the Sahara desert.

2. Write the area of the Sahara Desert in word form.

3. Which equation would you use to find the difference between the record-setting hottest and coldest temperatures?
   - **A.** 136 + 128.6 = 264.6
   - **B.** 128.6 − 136 = -7.4
   - **C.** 136 − 128.6 = 7.4
   - **D.** 134 − 95 = 39

4. The area of the United States is 3,537,441 square miles. Compare the area of the United States to the area of the Sahara Desert.

5. Using the correct equation in Question 3 as a model, calculate the number of degrees the temperature dropped in Browning, Montana, in 1 day.

6. Complete the number line below to show the **range** of temperatures in Verkhoyansk, Russia.

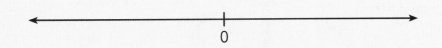

0

THIS GEODE ROCKS!

■ Check this out!

Largest Amethyst Geode

A geode is the only "cavity" your dentist might like you to have. It is a rock cavity filled with minerals! Amethyst is a purple rock mineral often found inside a geode. The world's Largest Amethyst Geode is 9 feet 10 inches long and 5 feet 10 inches wide. It weighs 28,600 pounds!

Amethysts can be found in many parts of the world. Brazil has large amethyst geodes. Great amounts of amethyst can also be found in Zambia. That country mines about 2,204,622 pounds of amethysts each year.

MORE AMAZING RECORDS

Largest Geode: The world's Largest Geode is a mineral-lined cave that is 26 feet long, 6 feet wide, and 6 feet high.

Largest Geoglyphs: A geoglyph is a large picture made with lines and rocks positioned on the ground. The world's Largest Geoglyphs are called the Nazca Lines—a group of figures that average 600 feet long. One arrow alone is more than 1,600 feet long! The figures show plants, animals, and shapes. Some people think the mysterious designs were created as a giant calendar.

You can see the record-setting geode on display in a natural history museum in Shandong, China. Aren't you glad that a dentist didn't try to fill this cavity?

Name_____ Date_____

■ Answer the questions. Show your work.

1. The world's Largest Amethyst Geode is 9 feet 10 inches long. What fraction of a foot is 10 inches equal to?

    A. $\frac{1}{10}$ of a foot

    B. $\frac{5}{6}$ of a foot

    C. $\frac{1}{2}$ of a foot

    D. $\frac{9}{10}$ of a foot

2. **Estimate** how many tons the world's Largest Amethyst Geode weighs.

3. How many more **inches** long is the world's Largest Amethyst Geode than it is wide?

4. Which equation shows the approximate **volume** of the world's Largest Geode in feet?
    A. 26 x 6 x 6 = 936 cubic feet
    B. 26 x 6 = 156 cubic feet
    C. 26 x 12 = 312 cubic feet
    D. 26 + 6 + 6 = 38 cubic feet

5. **Estimate** how many of the world's Largest Amethyst Geodes would equal the amount of amethysts mined in Zambia each year?

6. Compare the 1,600-**foot** arrow of the Nazca Lines to a 100-**yard** football field. About how many lengths of a football field would equal 1 of the arrows? Explain your thinking.

THIS WILL BLOW YOU AWAY!

■ Check this out!

Largest Measured Tornado

A tornado blew Dorothy to the Land of Oz in the fictional movie *The Wizard of Oz*. But, the world's Largest Measured Tornado is not fiction. The tornado happened on May 3, 1999, in Oklahoma. Its diameter was about 5,250 feet!

Tornadoes can spin at speeds of more than 300 miles per hour. And, they move along the ground at speeds of about 30 to 40 miles per hour.

So, how do weather scientists measure tornadoes? Joshua Wurman (USA) measured the record-breaking tornado using a mobile weather station. Wurman is known for studying extreme weather. This is definitely one record that is best just to read about!

MORE AMAZING RECORDS

Most Tornadoes in 1 Day: The record number of tornadoes in a 24-hour period is 148. On April 3–4, 1974, these tornadoes swept through the southern and midwestern United States. This part of the country is sometimes called Tornado Alley.

Most Tornadoes Sighted by 1 Person: Gene Moore of San Antonio, Texas, has seen more than 263 tornadoes in 30 years of storm chasing. On April 10, 1997, he saw 8 in a single day!

Name_____ Date_____

■ Answer the questions. Show your work.

1. Write **greater than**, **less than**, or **equal to** to complete the sentence.

The diameter of the world's Largest Tornado is _____ 1 mile.

2. A tornado that travels 30 miles per hour will travel _____ miles in 1.5 hours.

3. How long before January 1, 2010, did the world's Largest Tornado happen in years, months, and days?

4. If the diameter of a tornado were a perfect circle, which equation would you use to calculate the **circumference** of the tornado?
   A. 3.14 x 2,625 = circumference
   B. 3.14 x 6,890,625 = circumference
   C. 3.14 x 5,250 = circumference
   D. 5,250 ÷ 2 = circumference

5. If they came at an even rate, **about** how many tornadoes swept through Tornado Alley on April 3–4, 1974, each hour?

6. About how fast can a tornado spin **per second**? Explain your thinking.

GLOW-IN-THE-DARK BACTERIA?

■ Check this out!
Largest Area of Glowing Seawater

Glowing, eerie patches of seawater sound like science fiction. But, this patch of glowing seawater was real! It set the Guinness World Records™ record for the world's Largest Area of Glowing Seawater. The patch of water was more than 155 miles long. It had an area of about 5,400 square miles. That is about the size of the U.S. state of Connecticut!

In 1995, scientists saw a patch of glowing seawater in the Indian Ocean. They used satellite pictures to study it. Scientists think that it may have been caused by glow-in-the-dark bacteria. Sometimes, the bacteria grows on plants or fish. When the plants or fish get together in groups, they cause a patch of glowing sea!

MORE AMAZING RECORDS

Deepest Blue Hole: Dean's Blue Hole is 250 feet wide and 663 feet deep. It is at Turtle Cove on the Atlantic edge of the Bahamas. The blue hole contains 38.8 million cubic feet of water. This area is also the world's second-largest water-filled cavern.

Clearest Sea: The Weddell Sea off of Antarctica has the clearest water of any sea or ocean in the world. Scientists measure clarity by lowering a disc into the water until it can no longer be seen. In the Weddell Sea, the disc could still be seen at a depth of 262 feet!

■ Answer the questions. Show your work.

1. The measurement of the cubic feet of water in Dean's Blue Hole is **closest** to which amount?

    A. 37 million cubic feet

    B. $37\frac{1}{2}$ million cubic feet

    C. 39 million cubic feet

    D. $39\frac{1}{2}$ million cubic feet

2. How many **inches** deep did the disc reach in the Weddell Sea?

3. The depth of Dean's Blue Hole is **more than** _____ times the width of the hole.

4. Could a disc be seen at the bottom of Dean's Blue Hole? Explain your thinking.

5. **About** how many feet long was the Largest Area of Glowing Seawater?

6. **About** how many miles wide was the Largest Area of Glowing Seawater? Explain your thinking.

JOHNNY APPLESEED WOULD BE PROUD!

■ Check this out!

Most Trees Planted by a Team in 24 Hours

Johnny Appleseed planted apple trees throughout the United States. So, he would be proud of this team of 300 people from India. They worked together to plant 611,137 trees in Dungarpur Rajasthan, India. This event set the Guinness World Records™ record for the Most Trees Planted by a Team in 24 Hours.

The team started at 7:15 P.M. on August 11, 2009. They dug holes until 6:00 A.M. the next day. Then, they planted trees all day. They planted mostly fruit trees in order to help provide food for the local people. This team broke a world record and helped their community, all in a single day's work!

MORE AMAZING RECORDS

Most Trees Planted in a Public Park: When building Central Park in New York City, workers planted about 5 million trees. The park covers about 700 acres.

Most Palm Trees Planted in 10 Years: The world record for the Most Palm Trees Planted in 10 years is 42 million. The record was broken by the United Arab Emirates between 1999 and 2009.

Most Trees Planted at the Same Time: The Most Trees Planted at the Same Time is 938,007. On August 15, 2009, 169,920 people planted these trees throughout India.

Name_____ Date_____

■ Answer the questions. Show your work.

1. If each team member planted the same amount of trees during the 24 hours, **about** how many trees did each person plant?

2. It took _____ hours, _____ minutes for the team from India to dig the holes.

3. Order the tree-planting records from least amount of trees planted to greatest amount of trees planted.

    _____ Most Trees Planted by a Team in 24 Hours

    _____ Most Trees Planted in a Public Park

    _____ Most Palm Trees Planted in 10 Years

    _____ Most Trees Planted at the Same Time

4. How many **total** trees were planted during these 4 record-setting events?

5. If each acre of Central Park has the same number of trees, **estimate** the number of trees per acre.

6. Who planted more trees per person—the 300 people who planted 611,137 trees in 24 hours or the 169,920 people who planted 6,873,451 in 8 hours? Explain your thinking.

MARTIAN METEORITE MYSTERY

A rule to prevent forest fires... "SMOKEY'S

■ Check this out!

Largest Martian Meteorite

Meteorites are one of the mysteries of space. They are rocks that travel through space and land on Earth. Scientists do not know much about meteorites. When the meteorites are found, scientists try to piece together information about them.

The world's Largest Martian Meteorite weighs about 40 pounds. It came all the way from Mars! It was found on October 3, 1962. A farmer found it in a field in Nigeria. It made a crater that was 2 feet deep!

About 32 martian meteorites have been found. These pieces of rock help scientists learn more about our closest neighbor in the solar system.

MORE AMAZING RECORDS

Largest Meteorite (Not from Mars): The world's Largest Meteorite is 9 feet 8 inches long and 9 feet 4 inches wide. It weighs more than 130,000 pounds! It was found in 1920 in Namibia.

Largest Moon Meteorite: About 30 moon meteorites have been discovered on Earth. The world's Largest Moon Meteorite is Dar al Gani 400. It weighs 3.141 pounds. It was discovered in Libya in 1998.

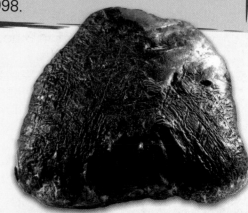

Name_____ Date_____

■ Answer the questions. Show your work.

1. The world's Largest Martian Meteorite weighs _____ **ounces**.

2. Write **greater than**, **less than**, or **equal to** to complete the sentence.

The size of martian meteorites is _____ the size of moon meteorites.

3. Based on the information in the passage, what is the **probability** of a meteorite falling into your yard?
  A. likely   **B.** unlikely
  C. impossible   **D.** certain

4. The world's Largest Meteorite is about how many times larger than the world's Largest Martian Meteorite?

5. The world's Largest Meteorite is shaped roughly like a rectangular prism. The surface area of the top of the meteorite is **about** how many square inches?

6. On the time line below, write the years that the 3 record-breaking meteorites were discovered. In between the dates, indicate the number of years that passed between each discovery.

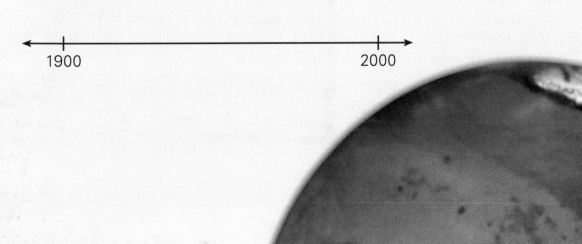

1900   2000

GIANT WAVES FROM NOWHERE

■ Check this out!

Earliest Proven Rogue Wave

Rogue waves rise out of nowhere, and they reach heights of at least 82 feet. That is about the height of an 8-story building! To be a rogue wave, a wave must be much higher than the waves in the same area. The Earliest Proven Rogue Wave entered the record books on January 1, 1995. It was 84 feet high! It struck in the North Sea. A special platform in the sea measured the huge wave.

Scientists guess that the tallest rogue wave could get to be as high as 198 feet. Large waves can reach about 30 feet. Most rogue waves average about 100 feet high. They are now believed to be more common than once thought.

MORE AMAZING RECORDS

Highest Wave: The world's Highest Wave was 112 feet high in the Pacific Ocean. People on a ship called the USS *Ramapo* measured it on the night of February 6-7, 1933. The wave happened during a hurricane that reached a speed of 78 miles per hour.

Most Surfers Riding the Same Wave: The record for the Most Surfers Riding the Same Wave is 110. They set the record during an event that was part of the Earthwave Beach Festival in Cape Town, South Africa, to raise awareness of climate change.

Name_____ Date_____

■ Answer the questions. Show your work.

1. How much **higher** was the world's Highest Wave than the Earliest Proven Rogue Wave?

2. "Hang ten" is a surfing phrase that refers to 10 toes on a surfboard. How many toes rode the wave ridden by the Most Surfers Riding the Same Wave?

3. A 1-story building is **about** how many feet tall?
    A. 82 feet
    B. 41 feet
    C. 10 feet
    D. 820 feet

4. Most rogue waves average about _____ **times** the size of large waves.

5. What is the **probability** of seeing a rogue wave while surfing? Explain your thinking.

6. The world's Highest Wave was about what **percentage** higher than the average rogue wave? Explain your thinking.

A LOT LONGER THAN A FOOT LONG

■ Check this out!

Longest Loaf of Bread

Some sandwich shops sell foot-long sandwiches for $5.00. A sandwich made with the world's Longest Loaf of Bread, however, would have cost $19,875.00 because it was 3,975 feet long!

The Guinness World Records™ record-breaking loaf of bread was baked in Portugal on July 10, 2005. The bread was baked in an oven that was almost 33 feet long. It was pulled through the oven using a steel cable and rollers. It took almost 60 hours to bake.

More than 100 bakers helped with the event. The loaf of bread fed more than 15,000 people. It raised money for local firefighters and the Red Cross. It helped raise $13,204.00!

MORE AMAZING RECORDS

Largest Bagel: The world's Largest Bagel weighed 868 pounds! It was made by Brueggers Bagels and was displayed at the New York State Fair on August 27, 2004.

Largest Pizza: The world's Largest Pizza ever baked weighed 26,883 pounds! It was made at Norwood Hypermarket in South Africa on December 8, 1990. It measured 122 feet 8 inches in diameter.

Largest Pretzel: The world's Largest Pretzel weighed 842 pounds! It measured 36 feet 10 inches in length. It was 10 feet 2 inches wide.

Name_____ Date_____

■ Answer the questions. Show your work.

1. The world's Largest Loaf of Bread raised $13,204.00. Write this dollar amount in word form.

2. Which equation shows how long the world's Longest Loaf of Bread was in inches?
- **A.** 3,975 x 10 = 39,750 inches
- **B.** 3,975 ÷ 12 = 331.25 inches
- **C.** 3,975 x 12 = 47,700 inches
- **D.** 3,975 x 16 = 63,600 inches

3. How much more did the world's Largest Pizza weigh than the world's Largest Bagel and the world's Largest Pretzel combined?

4. If each piece of the world's Longest Loaf of Bread were equal, **about** how long would each person's piece be?

5. An average bagel weighs about 1 ounce. How many people could the world's Largest Bagel feed? Explain your thinking.

6. If the world's Largest Pizza were sliced into **eighths** in typical wedge-shaped slices, how long would 1 slice of pizza be? Explain your thinking.

LONG MAY SHE WAVE

■ Check this out!

Largest Human National Flag

A national flag is a symbol for its country. One special flag set a record for being the world's Largest Human National Flag. It took 21,726 people to form this flag!

The flag was made at the Flags of Harmony and Unity event. The event was planned by the Hong Kong Polytechnic University. It was held on September 23, 2007.

MORE AMAZING RECORDS

Largest Human Logo: On July 24, 1999, a group of 34,309 people in Portugal created the world's Largest Human Logo. The people formed a soccer player kicking the ball.

Largest Human Rainbow: On September 18, 2004, a group of 30,365 people in the Philippines gathered to create the world's Largest Human Rainbow.

The goal was to have 20,000 people make up the flag, but even more people came! Each person was given a board, and each board had a number and a color. Everyone stood according to the board number. Together, the boards created the flag of Hong Kong, China.

Name_____ Date_____

■ **Answer the questions. Show your work.**

1. How many **more** people helped set the record for the world's Largest Human National Flag than the goal of 20,000?

2. How many **more** people created the world's Largest Human Logo than the world's Largest Human National Flag?

3. Order the records below from the **least** to the **greatest** based on the number of people who helped break the records.

_____ Largest Human National Flag   _____ Largest Human Logo

_____ Largest Human Rainbow

4. _____ years, _____ days passed between setting the record for the Largest Human Rainbow and setting the record for the Largest Human Flag.

5. How many people would be needed to break the record for the world's Largest Human National Flag if the goal were to beat the record by 3 times as many people?

6. **Estimate** how the 21,726 people may have been organized to create the world's Largest Human National Flag. How many rows and how many people in each row might there have been?

HOW WOULD YOU LIKE YOUR EGGS?

■ Check this out!

Most Eggs Crushed with the Head in 1 Minute

Would you like your eggs fried, scrambled, or crushed with your head? Anjul Tomar (India) wanted his crushed with his head! He did this to set the world record for the Most Eggs Crushed with the Head in 1 Minute. He crushed 120 eggs! Tomar set this record on May 17, 2009, in Delhi, India.

Tomar broke the record by lining up the eggs along the edge of a table. He then moved down the table, crushing each egg with his head.

Tomar was born on July 19, 1992. Who knew that one day he would crush a world record!

MORE AMAZING RECORDS

Most Corn Husked in 1 Minute by a Team of 4: The record for the Most Corn Husked in 1 Minute by a Team of 4 is 17 ears!

Most Almonds Cracked in 3 Minutes: The record for the Most Almonds Cracked in 3 Minutes is 4. The record was broken to support The Rainbow Trust Children's Charity in Barcelona, Spain, on May 5, 2006.

Most Potatoes Peeled in 45 Minutes by a Team of 5: The record for the Most Potatoes Peeled in 45 Minutes by a Team of 5 is 1,064 pounds 6 ounces.

Name_____ Date_____

■ Answer the questions. Show your work.

1. On average, how many eggs did Tomar crush per second?

2. Order the 4 records from page 60 from **least** to **greatest** based on the number of food items crushed, husked, cracked, or peeled in 1 minute. (Assume that a typical potato weighs about 1/2 pound.)

3. In days, months, and years, how old was Tomar when he set his record?

4. Based on the record for cracking almonds, how many seconds did it take to crack 1 almond?

5. Based on the record for husking corn, **estimate** how long it took for 1 person to husk 1 ear of corn. Explain your thinking.

6. Estimate how many pounds of potatoes each person on the team peeled each minute.

GREAT GOBS OF GREEN GOO!

© 2010 Viacom International Inc. All Rights Reserved. Nickelodeon, Slime Time Live and all related titles, logos and characters are trademarks of Viacom International Inc. Photograph by Tom Hurst.

■ Check this out!

Most People Slimed at the Same Time

The TV station Nickelodeon is known for pouring gobs of green goo over people's heads. So, this Guinness World Records™ record is for the Most People Slimed at the Same Time. An amazing 762 people were slimed to break this record!

The record was set on October 27, 2003. It happened as part of Nickelodeon's *Slime Time Live* show. The 762 guests were slimed with about 150 gallons of the green goo. The slime was fired into the air by 10 cannons. It then rained down on the screaming crowd. Can you imagine cleaning up that mess? Hopefully, they had a big hose!

MORE AMAZING RECORDS

Most People Slimed in 3 Minutes: The record for Most People Slimed in 3 Minutes is 24. Paul O'Grady and his guests, Davina McCall and Richard Arnold (all UK), broke this record on June 2, 2008.

Most People Getting a Mud Treatment: The record for Most People Getting a Mud Treatment is 50. The event happened on March 28, 2009, in Germany.

Name_____ Date_____

■ Answer the questions. Show your work.

1. To calculate how many ounces of slime were dumped on the 762 guests, what **additional information** do you need to know that was not provided in the passage?

    A. how many gallons of slime were dumped

    B. how many ounces are in a gallon

    C. how much the 762 guests weighed

    D. how much slime got on each guest

2. How much time passed between when 762 guests were slimed and when 50 people got a mud treatment?

    _____ years, _____ months, _____ days

3. How many quarts of slime did **each** cannon fire?

4. Based on the record for Most People Slimed in 3 Minutes, **about** how long did it take to slime 1 person?

5. About how many **minutes** would it take to slime the 762 guests 1 at a time? Explain your thinking.

6. If each of the 762 guests received the same amount of slime, **about** how many ounces of slime did each guest get?

SUPERHEROES SET SUPER RECORD

■ Check this out!

Most People Dressed as Superheroes

Superheroes do amazing things. But, these ordinary people set a super record. A group of 1,016 people set a record for the Most People Dressed as Superheroes! They set this record on August 29, 2009.

Setting this record was just one event planned for the day. Other events included a 13-mile half marathon and a 1-mile fun run. The event planners were raising money for the Children's Hospital in Hanover, New Hampshire.

Participants came dressed as many different superheroes. These real people were real superheroes. They helped raise about $225,000.00 for the Children's Hospital!

MORE AMAZING RECORDS

Most People Dressed as Sunflowers: The record for the Most People Dressed as Sunflowers is 116. This record was set on August 13, 2008.

Most People Dressed as Nurses: The record for the Most People Dressed as Nurses is 116. This record was set on October 11, 2008.

Most People Dressed as Video Game Characters: The record for the Most People Dressed as Video Game Characters is 376. This record was set on May 23, 2009.

Name_____ Date_____

■ Answer the questions. Show your work.

1. How much **more** money would the group of superheroes have to raise to reach $1 million?

2. How many **fewer** people dressed as video game characters than as superheroes?

3. If the superheroes held hands and made a line, and the average arm span of each person were 3 feet, how long would the line be?
- **A.** 3,348 feet
- **B.** 3,048 feet
- **C.** 1,038 feet
- **D.** 3,338 feet

4. How many people **altogether** dressed up to set all 4 of these records?

5. How long is a **full** marathon? Explain your thinking.

6. _____ **days** passed between breaking the records for the Most People Dressed as Sunflowers and the Most People Dressed as Nurses.

ON TOP OF THE WORLD

■ Check this out!

Highest Altitude Hotel

This hotel takes being on top of the world to a new level. The Hotel Everest View broke the record for being the Highest Altitude Hotel in the world. It is 13,000 feet above sea level!

The hotel is located in Sagarmatha National Park, Nepal. It got its name for its view of Mount Everest. It also boasts amazing views of the Himalayas. To get to the hotel, you must make a 2- or 3-day hike!

The hotel was built with many comforts. It has electricity, tiled showers, flush toilets, and even a volleyball court. The next time you are feeling a little down, stay at this hotel. It is sure to help you feel on top of the world again!

MORE AMAZING RECORDS

Highest Altitude by a Single Kite: Richard P. Synergy (Canada) flew a kite to an altitude of about 14,509 feet. The kite had a wingspan of 30 feet, and it was 18 feet tall. It flew on a 270-pound line with a diameter of 3/32 inches.

Highest Altitude by an Aircraft: The world's highest flight is 123,523 feet. It was set by Alexandr Fedotov (former USSR) flying a MIG-25 Foxbat. The Foxbat is a military aircraft that can take off and reach 114,000 feet in about 4 minutes.

Highest Altitude by Car: The world record for driving to the Highest Altitude by Car is 21,942 feet. Gonzalo Bravo and Eduardo Canales (both Chile) broke this record on the slopes of a volcano in Chile.

Name_____ Date_____

■ Answer the questions. Show your work.

1. Number the altitude records below from **highest** to **lowest**.

_____ Hotel Everest View   _____ kite   _____ aircraft   _____ car

2. Is the altitude of the Hotel Everest View **more than** or **less than** 3 miles above sea level? Explain your thinking.

3. Draw a picture of the highest flying kite showing the **proportion** of wingspan to height.

4. How long of a rope would be needed to reach from the Hotel Everest View to 12,700 feet **below** sea level?

5. About how many times higher did the Foxbat fly than the highest flying kite?

6. About how many feet per second could the Foxbat climb in altitude?

TEXTING ONE, TWO, THREE

■ Check this out!

Fastest Text Message while Blindfolded

Texting is a quick way for people to stay in touch. Elliot Nicholls (New Zealand) broke the Guinness World Records™ record for the Fastest Text Message while Blindfolded! He tapped this message in record time:

> The razor-toothed piranhas of the genera Serrasalmus and Pygocentrus are the most ferocious freshwater fish in the world. In reality they seldom attack a human.

On the same day in 2007, Nicholls broke the record twice. First, he broke the earlier record of 1 minute, 26 seconds. It took him only 51 seconds. He tried again and broke his own record, tapping the message in only 45.09 seconds!

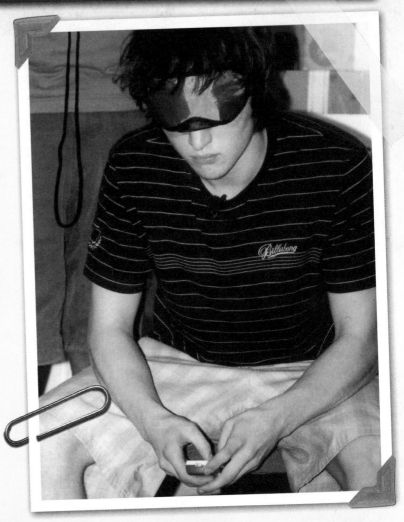

MORE AMAZING RECORDS

Fastest Text Message: The world's Fastest Text Message took 37.28 seconds. Sonja Kristiansen (Norway) broke this record on November 14, 2009. She finished the official 160-character message more than 20 seconds before her challenger!

Fastest Text Message in Arabic: The world's Fastest Text Message in Arabic took 43.44 seconds. Ali Jaffar Al Ansari (United Arab Emirates) broke this record on November 29, 2008.

Fastest Text Message Sent around the World: On May 22, 2005, a text message was sent around the world. It was forwarded to cell phones in 6 countries on 6 continents and finally back to the original phone. The message was received by the original phone after only 2 minutes, 28 seconds.

Name_____ Date_____

■ **Answer the questions. Show your work.**

1. How much faster did Nicholls tap the text message on his second try?

2. On his first try, by how many seconds did Nicholls beat the previous record?

3. How much faster did Kristiansen tap without a blindfold than Nicholls tapped with a blindfold?

4. Assuming the message was the same, which is faster—to text in Arabic or to text blindfolded? Explain your thinking.

5. On average, for the text sent around the world, **about** how many seconds did it take to receive and send the text message in each country?

6. About how many characters did Kristiansen tap per second? Explain your thinking.

NOT YOUR $5 PIZZA

■ Check this out!

Most Expensive Pizza

Pizza is usually tasty and fairly inexpensive. At some restaurants, you can get a whole pizza for only $5.00. But, one restaurant in London, called Maze, broke the record for creating the world's Most Expensive Pizza. Each pizza sells for $178.00!

This gourmet pizza has a thin crust and is topped with onions, mushrooms, and 2 types of cheese. So, what makes this pizza so special and expensive? It is topped with wild lettuce and shavings of white truffle, a rare fungus. Truffles are hard to find, which makes them very expensive. The white truffle used on this pizza costs about $1,000.00 per pound! Would you trade a cheese pizza for a fungus pizza at any price?

MORE AMAZING RECORDS

The Most Expensive Hamburger: The world's Most Expensive Hamburger was served in London. It sold for $186.00! And, guess what the secret ingredient was—truffles!

Most Expensive Sandwich: The world's Most Expensive Sandwich is the von Essen Platinum Club Sandwich, created by Chef Daniel Galmiche (UK). You can enjoy this sandwich for just $200.00!

Most Expensive Box of Cherries: The world's Most Expensive Box of Cherries sold for $31,771.00 in Australia. It was sold to benefit a charity.

Name_____ Date_____

■ Answer the questions. Show your work.

1. How much would you **spend** before taxes and tip at Maze to buy everyone in a family of four 1 record-breaking pizza each?

2. How much money could you **save** by purchasing the record-breaking hamburger instead of the record-breaking sandwich?

3. If you had $1,000.00 and you purchased 1 record-breaking pizza, 2 record-breaking hamburgers, and 2 record-setting sandwiches, how much money would you have left over?

4. An average tip at a nice restaurant is 20 percent. How much should you leave as a tip for purchasing 1 record-breaking pizza?

5. If the world's Most Expensive Box of Cherries had 2 dozen cherries in the box, **estimate** the cost of each cherry.

6. If you add 5 percent for taxes and 20 percent for tip, would the entire bill for a party of 8 eating the Most Expensive Hamburgers be **more than** or **less than** $1,500.00? Explain your thinking.

FOR A PINK CAUSE

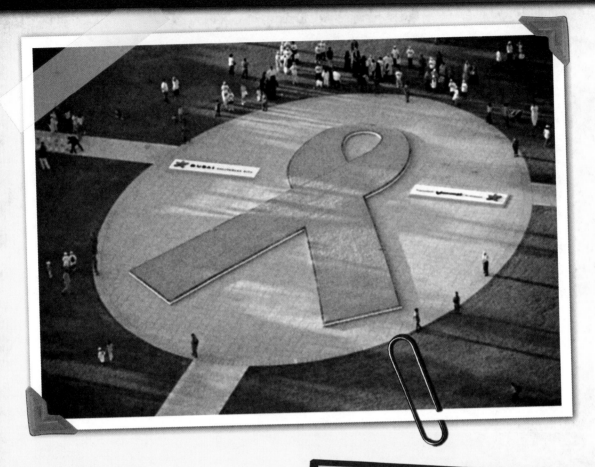

■ Check this out!

Largest Awareness Ribbon Made of Flowers

Many people wear ribbons to show support for many good causes. Wearing a pink ribbon shows support for breast cancer research. But, 1 big pink ribbon is unique. The world's Largest Awareness Ribbon Made of Flowers set a record on November 16, 2007. It was 94 feet 2 inches long. The ribbon was made from 105,000 pink carnations.

The first pink ribbons to support breast cancer were worn in 1990. People wore them at the Race for the Cure event. This is a huge fund-raising event for cancer research. Hopefully one day, a cure for breast cancer will be found. Until then, can you think of a better way to use 105,000 pink carnations?

MORE AMAZING RECORDS

Largest Flower Mural: The world's Largest Flower Mural was created on August 7, 2001, in the Netherlands by 1,250 people. They glued 770,000 fresh dahlias to 900 panels. The mural was 19.78 feet tall and 1,016.86 feet long. Its area was 20,117 square feet!

Largest Flower Carpet: The world's Largest Flower Carpet was 81,164 square feet. It was 400.1 feet wide and 202.82 feet long. It was created using red, white, and blue delphiniums.

Name_____ Date_____

■ Answer the questions. Show your work.

1. Which is the correct way to write the number of pink carnations used in the world's Largest Awareness Ribbon Made of Flowers?

    A. one hundred and five thousand

    B. one hundred five million

    C. one hundred fifty thousand

    D. one hundred five thousand

2. How many more dahlias were used to create the mural than carnations were used to create the ribbon?

3. The pink carnation ribbon was _____ **inches** long.

4. Which was larger—the world's Largest Flower Mural or the world's Largest Flower Carpet? What is the difference?

5. What is the **perimeter** of the world's Largest Flower Mural in feet?

6. **Estimate** about how many carnations were used per inch in the Largest Awareness Ribbon Made of Flowers. Explain your thinking.

AN AMAZING MAZE

■ Check this out!

Largest Temporary Corn Maze

Do you like to work mazes? This record-breaking maze was so big that you could walk through it. The world's Largest Temporary Corn Maze covered 40.489 acres!

Mark Cooley (USA) created the maze. Cooley has been making corn mazes since 2005. The record-breaking maze was open from September to November 2007. It was located in Dixon, California.

How did Cooley make this maze? Using math! With the help of a computer program, he made a grid. Each box of the grid represented 5 square feet of the cornfield. Then, Cooley drew the path. He made sure to include plenty of twists and turns to make the maze interesting and fun!

MORE AMAZING RECORDS

Largest Tree Maze: The world's Largest Tree Maze is the Samsø Labyrinten. It has an area of 645,835 square feet. Its path is 16,830 feet 8 inches long. The maze is located north of Samsø Island in Denmark.

Largest Hedge Maze: The world's Largest Hedge Maze is the Pineapple Garden Maze at the Dole Plantation in Wahiawa, Hawaii. It has a total area of 3.15 acres. Its path is 2.46 miles long.

Largest Ice Maze: The world's Largest Ice Maze was the Arctic Glacier Ice Maze in Buffalo, New York. It had an area of 12,855.68 square feet.

Name_____ Date_____

■ Answer the questions. Show your work.

1. How much **larger** was the corn maze than the hedge maze in acres?

2. Which of the following shows the correct order of the four record-breaking mazes from **smallest** area to **largest** area?
   - **A.** ice, hedge, tree, corn
   - **B.** corn, tree, hedge, ice
   - **C.** ice, tree, hedge, corn
   - **D.** hedge, ice, tree, corn

3. How much **smaller** was the ice maze than the tree maze?

4. An acre is equal to 43,560 square feet. Estimate the area of the corn maze in square feet.

5. **Estimate** the difference between the length of the path in the tree maze and the length of the path in the hedge maze. Explain your thinking.

6. **About** how many 5-foot square boxes were in the grid Cooley used to plan the corn maze? (Hint: For easy dividing, calculate the number of boxes that would be in 100 square feet. Then, adjust your answer by multiplying by that number of boxes.)

COINS FOR A CAUSE

■ Check this out!

Most Money Raised for a Charity in Coins

Have you ever given coins to help others? The most coins ever collected for charity was 666,809. In 1998, they had a total value of 44,395,727.96 escudos. (The *escudo* is the money formerly used in Portugal.) This is the same as about $273,565.00!

The coins were counted at the Expo 98 in Lisbon, Portugal. The coins were donated to UNICEF.

UNICEF stands for the United Nations International Children's Emergency Fund. This fund was started to help children after World War II. Today, UNICEF helps children in more than 78 countries. It helps more than 15.2 million children receive food, medicine, education, and other important services. What a great way to use those extra coins!

MORE AMAZING RECORDS

Most Money Made from Recycled Bottles and Cans: Stanley Chapman (USA) collected 578,961 bottles and cans. The total cash he collected from his recycling efforts was $57,896.00.

Greatest Prize Money Won on Radio: Clare Barwick of Worthing, West Sussex, became the United Kingdom's first radio quiz show millionaire. She won an amount equal to $1,600,000.00.

Name_____ Date_____

■ Answer the questions. Show your work.

1. Which of the following is the world record number of coins collected for charity?

   A. six hundred sixty-six thousand eight hundred nine

   B. six million six hundred six eight hundred nine

   C. six thousand sixty-six eight hundred nine

   D. six hundred sixty-six eight hundred nine

2. Use **expanded notation** to write the number of children UNICEF helps each year.

3. What was the total dollar amount collected in coins and recycling?

4. How much more money would need to be collected in coins and recycling to equal the amount of the radio prize money?

5. **About** how much was each bottle and can worth when Chapman recycled it?

6. In 1998, **about** how many escudos were equal to 1 dollar? Explain your thinking.

PEDAL POWER

■ Check this out!

Greatest Distance on a Human-Powered Vehicle in 24 Hours

Have you ever heard of a human-powered vehicle? If you have ever ridden a bike you have! This record-setting human-powered vehicle is like a bike—with the works!

Greg Kolodziejzyk (Canada) used this vehicle to break the world record for the Greatest Distance on a Human-Powered Vehicle in 24 Hours. The previous record was 634 miles. Kolodziejzyk traveled 647 miles! He set this record on a track on July 18, 2006.

Kolodziejzyk designed and built this bike. He named it *Critical Power*. The shape was made to travel fast. The bike can reach speeds of 62 miles per hour, and it averages about 31 miles per hour. Can you imagine riding a bike for 24 hours?

MORE AMAZING RECORDS

Greatest Distance by Pedal Boat: The record for the Greatest Distance by Pedal Boat was set by Kenichi Horie (Japan). He pedaled 4,660 miles from Honolulu, Hawaii, to Okinawa, Japan. He left Hawaii on October 30, 1992. He reached Okinawa on February 17, 1993.

Greatest Distance Flown in a Wingsuit: Expert skydiver Adrian Nicholas (UK) flew a record 10 miles in a wingsuit. He jumped out of a plane at 33,850 feet. He flew for 4 minutes, 55 seconds. He opened his parachute only 500 feet from the ground!

Name_____ Date_____

■ **Answer the questions. Show your work.**

1. By how much did Kolodziejzyk break the previous record?

2. Which equation shows how far Kolodziejzyk would travel if he were to maintain 62 miles per hour for an entire 24 hours.

    A. 62 x 60 x 24 = 89,280 miles   **B.** 62 x 24 = 1,488 miles

    C. (62 ÷ 24) x 60 = 154.9 miles   **D.** 62 x 24 x 2 = 2,976 miles

3. Use words to write the number of miles Horie pedaled.

4. It took Horie _____ months, _____ days to travel from Honolulu, Hawaii, to Okinawa, Japan.

5. How many seconds did Nicholas fly through the air?

6. **Estimate** how many days it would take Kolodziejzyk to pedal the same distance Horie pedaled by boat. Explain your thinking.

A MIGHTY GRAND DAM

■ Check this out!

Highest Concrete Dam

Dams are mighty structures built to store water for future use. The first dams were created using rocks and sticks. As communities grew larger, so did the need to store more water. People started to build large concrete dams.

Today, the Grande Dixence Dam in Switzerland is the world's Highest Concrete Dam. It is 935 feet high! That is about the same height as 3 football fields standing end to end. The dam is 2,297 feet long. That is almost 1/2 mile long! It took about 210,400,000 cubic feet of concrete to build. That is one grand dam!

MORE AMAZING RECORDS

Highest Dam: The Nurek Dam in Tajikistan is the world's Highest Dam. It towers 984 feet high. It is an earth-filled dam.

Largest Concrete Dam: The world's Largest Concrete Dam is the Grand Coulee Dam on the Columbia River in Washington. It is 550 feet high and 4,173 feet long. It is made of 285,760,000 cubic feet of concrete!

Longest Dam: The world's Longest Dam is the Kiev Dam in the Ukraine. It is 25.6 miles long!

Name_____ Date_____

■ Answer the questions. Show your work.

1. How much higher is the Nurek Dam than the Grande Dixence Dam?

2. How much more concrete was used to build the Grand Coulee Dam than the Grande Dixence Dam?

3. The Kiev Dam is about _____ feet long. **Estimate** to find the answer.

4. What is the **average** of the heights of the Grande Dixence, the Nurek, and the Grand Coulee dams?

5. Based on the information provided, what can you **conclude** about the height of the Kiev Dam? Explain your thinking.

6. On a separate sheet of paper, draw a picture showing the **relative lengths** in miles of the Grande Dixence Dam, the Grand Coulee Dam, and the Kiev Dam.

POWERED BY THE SUN

■ Check this out!

Longest Journey by Solar Electric Vehicle

People are looking for a solution to the problem of pollution. Is the answer a solar electric car?

A team from the University of Waterloo in Canada thinks so. They broke the Guinness World Records™ record for the Longest Journey by Solar Electric Vehicle. The team traveled 9,364 miles through Canada and the United States.

The car was named *Midnight Sun VII*. The first *Midnight Sun* was built in 1990. *Midnight Sun VII* left Waterloo on August 7, 2004. The trip ended in Ottawa, Canada, on September 15, 2004. That is a long time to travel pollution free!

MORE AMAZING RECORDS

Fastest Crossing of the Atlantic by Solar-Powered Boat: The world's Fastest Crossing of the Atlantic by Solar-Powered Boat is 29 days. The crew of the *sun21* broke this record.

Fastest Solar-Powered Vehicle: The record-breaking speed of the world's Fastest Solar-Powered Vehicle is 48.71 miles per hour. Molly Brennan (USA) broke this record while driving a car named *Sunraycer*. She raced a distance of 1,950 miles, and she averaged a speed of 41.6 miles per hour.

Name_____ Date_____

■ Answer the questions. Show your work.

1. It took the solar-powered boat **almost** 1 _____ to cross the
   Atlantic Ocean.

   A. day

   B. week

   C. month

   D. year

2. Is the speed of the world's Fastest Solar-Powered Vehicle **closer** to
   48 miles per hour or 49 miles per hour? Explain your thinking.

3. How many days did the trip from Waterloo to Ottawa take in the
   Midnight Sun VII?

4. How much farther did the *Midnight Sun VII* travel than the *Sunraycer?*

5. **About** how many miles did the *Midnight Sun VII* travel each day?

6. If the *Midnight Sun VII* traveled at the record-breaking rate of 48.71 miles per hour,
   estimate how many hours it would take for it to travel its record-breaking distance.
   Explain your thinking.

READY FOR TAKEOFF!

■ Check this out!

Farthest Flight by a Paper Aircraft

On September 6, 2003, Stephen Krieger (USA) flew an airplane 207 feet 4 inches. Why is that special? The airplane was made from a single sheet of paper and some tape! Krieger flew the airplane inside of an airplane hangar. He broke the record for the Farthest Flight by a Paper Airplane! Krieger was 15 years old at the time.

When he was 11, Krieger set what he thought was an impossible goal. His goal was to fly a paper airplane the farthest distance in the world. Then 2 years later, he came up with a record-breaking design. It took him another 2 years to make it just right.

MORE AMAZING RECORDS

Largest Paper Airplane: The world's Largest Paper Airplane has a wingspan of 45 feet 10 inches. In 1995, it flew 114 feet 2 inches!

Most Accurate Paper Airplane Flyer: Fumihiro Uno (Japan) flew 6 paper airplanes into a bucket from a distance of 9 feet 10 inches.

Longest Flight Time of a Paper Airplane: The longest time a paper airplane has stayed in the air is 27.9 seconds.

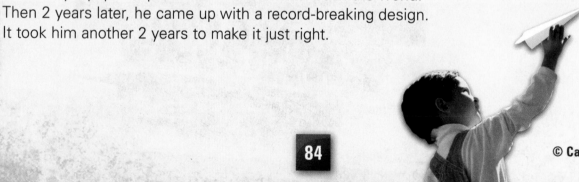

Name_____ Date_____

■ Answer the questions. Show your work.

1. How far did Krieger's airplane fly in inches?

    A. 641 inches

    B. 2,448 inches

    C. 688 inches

    D. 2,452 inches

2. How much **farther** did Krieger's airplane fly than the world's Largest Paper Airplane?

3. How **old** was Krieger on September 6, 2010?

4. What was the total distance the 6 most accurate paper airplanes flew **altogether**?

5. The world's Longest Flight Time of a Paper Airplane lasted **about** what fraction of a minute?

    A. $\frac{1}{3}$ of a minute   **B.** $\frac{1}{4}$ of a minute

    C. $\frac{1}{2}$ of a minute   **D.** $\frac{1}{6}$ of a minute

6. About how many times farther did the world's Largest Paper Airplane fly than its wingspan? Do you think that's very far? Explain your thinking.

A HOD-HEADED MAN

■ Check this out!

Heaviest Weight Balanced on the Head

Are you hod-headed? John Evans (UK) is! A hod is a trough used to carry bricks. And, because Evans has held 101 bricks on his head, this title is accurate. The 101 bricks were enough for Evans to break the record for the Heaviest Weight Balanced on the Head. The bricks weighed 416 pounds!

Evans broke the record on December 24, 1997. To break the record, he had to hold the weight for 10 seconds.

Evans' neck measures 24 inches around. At the age of 18, he started carrying bricks at a building site. He found that he could carry the most bricks by balancing bricks using a "hod" hat!

MORE AMAZING RECORDS

Heaviest Weight Balanced on the Feet: The world's Heaviest Weight Balanced on the Feet was 573.86 pounds. Li Chunying (China) balanced a large ceramic pot with 2 people on it. He broke this world record on November 20, 2009.

Heaviest Weight Balanced on the Teeth: The world's Heaviest Weight Balanced on the Teeth is 140 pounds. The record was set by Frank Simon (UK). He balanced a refrigerator on his teeth for 10 seconds!

Name_____ Date_____

■ Answer the questions. Show your work.

1. Which tool would be the best for measuring around Evans' neck?
    A. ruler
    B. yardstick
    C. measuring tape
    D. protractor

2. **About** how much did each of Evans' bricks weigh?

3. How many more pounds did Chunying balance on his feet than Evans balanced on his head?

4. Evans' head can balance **about** _____ times more weight than Simon's teeth.

5. On the number line below, show where 573.86 pounds is between 573 and 574 pounds.

573   574

6. **Estimate** the weight of each of the 2 people and the ceramic pot that Chunying balanced on his feet. Explain your thinking.

A NAIL-BITING RECORD—NOT!

■ Check this out!

Longest Fingernails on 1 Hand

Do you bite your fingernails? Shridhar Chillal of India does not have that habit. He broke the Guinness World Records™ record for having the Longest Fingernails on 1 Hand. His 5 nails measured a total of 23 feet 1.5 inches!

Chillal's fingernails were measured on February 4, 2004. His thumbnail measured 62.2 inches, his index fingernail measured 51.6 inches, and his middle fingernail measured 54.3 inches. His ring fingernail was 55.1 inches, and his little fingernail was 54.3 inches. Chillal last cut his fingernails in 1952! Fingernails grow about 0.02 inches per week.

MORE AMAZING RECORDS

Longest Fingernails on a Female: The world's Longest Fingernails on a Female belonged to Lee Redmond (USA). She grew them to a total length of 28 feet 4.5 inches. She started growing them in 1979 and broke the world record in 2008. Her longest nail was on her right thumb. The nail measured 2 feet 11 inches!

Longest Fingernails on a Male: The longest fingernails on a male belonged to Melvin Boothe (USA). His nails had a combined length of 32 feet 3.8 inches. He broke the world record on May 30, 2009. His longest nail measured 45 inches!

Chillal decided to grow the fingernails on his left hand. He has had to use his right hand to do his everyday work. So, maybe Chillal's bad habit is *not* biting his nails!

Name_____ Date_____

■ Answer the questions. Show your work.

1. Chillal's 5 nails measured a total of _____ **inches**.

2. Which equation shows how to find the average length of Chillal's fingernails?

    A. 277.5 inches ÷ 5 = 55.5 inches

    B. 23 feet ÷ 5 = 4.6 inches

    C. 5 x 23.15 feet = 115.75 inches

    D. 23 feet 1.5 inches ÷ 10 = 27.75 inches

3. For how many more years did Chillal grow his nails before breaking the world record than Redmond grew hers before breaking the world record?

4. If fingernails grow about 0.02 inches per week, how long would a fingernail be in 5 weeks? Complete the table to solve the problem.

Week	Inches
1	0.02
2	
3	
4	
5	

5. Using the **pattern** from the table in Question 4, how many weeks would it take to grow a fingernail 1 inch?

6. If you **rounded** all of the measurements of Chillal's nails to the nearest whole inch, how would that affect the total measurement?

SENDING THE VERY TALLEST

■ Check this out!

Tallest Flower Arrangement

Flower arrangements come in all different shapes and sizes. One tower broke the record for the world's Tallest Flower Arrangement. It was 80 feet 1 inch high. It was made of chrysanthemums.

This flower arrangement is named for the Tengwangge Tower. It was on display at the Chrysanthemum Exhibition in China. It was measured on November 23, 2007.

Chrysanthemums have grown in China for more than 3,000 years. They are a popular flower in the United States too. They grow easily and stay fresh longer than most flowers. The next time you send flowers, do not just send them the very best—send them the very tallest!

MORE AMAZING RECORDS

Tallest Structure Built with Interlocking Plastic Bricks in 1 Minute: The world's Tallest Structure Built with Interlocking Plastic Bricks in 1 Minute is 65 bricks tall. It was built by Denise Russell of the United Kingdom.

Largest Canned Food Structure: The world's Largest Canned Food Structure was made of 115,527 cans. It was built by Disney VoluntEARS™ at Walt Disney World in Florida. The structure took 4 days to build. It was 49 feet 3 inches long and 16 feet 4 inches wide. It stood 4 feet 11 inches high.

Name_____ Date_____

■ Answer the questions. Show your work.

1. **True** or **False**—The world's Tallest Flower Arrangement is equal to 960 inches.

2. A 1-story house is about 13 feet tall. The world's Tallest Flower Arrangement is **about** the

same height as _____ 1-story houses.

3. If Russell continued building the plastic brick structure at the same **rate**, how tall would it be in 5 minutes? Complete the **table** to solve the problem.

Minutes	Bricks
1	65
2	
3	
4	
5	

4. An average can of food is about 4 inches tall. **About** how many cans high was the Largest Canned Food Structure?

5. If the world's Tallest Flower Arrangement were to use 3 chrysanthemums **per inch**, how many chrysanthemums tall would the arrangement be?

6. If each plastic brick were 1 inch high, **about** how long would it take to make a plastic brick structure the same height as the world's Tallest Flower Arrangement?

MORE THAN MOST

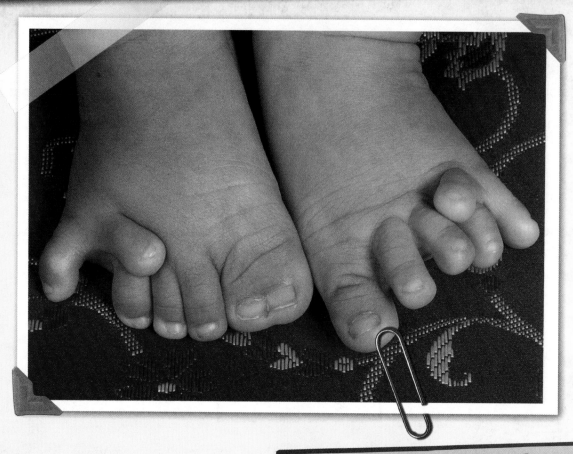

■ Check this out!

Most Fingers and Toes on a Living Person

Most people have 10 fingers and 10 toes. But, that is not the case for these record-holders! These 2 extraordinary people share the world record for having the Most Fingers and Toes on a Living Person. They were both born with 12 fingers and 13 toes!

MORE AMAZING RECORDS

Longest Toenails: Since 1982, Louise Hollis (USA) has been growing her toenails. When measured in 1991, the combined length of all 10 toenails was 87 inches.

Longest Toes: The world's Longest Toes belonged to Matthew McGrory (USA). His big toes each measured 5 inches long. His little toes each measured 1.5 inches long.

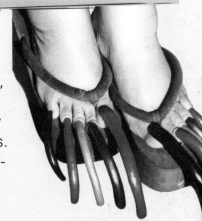

Pranamya Menaria and Devendra Harne (both India) were born with a condition called *polydactyly*. Harne was born January 9, 1995, and Menaria was born August 10, 2005. Polydactyly causes people to have extra fingers and/or toes. The condition can run in the family and is fairly common. It happens in about 1 out of every 1,000 births. Usually though, it happens in only 1 hand or 1 foot. So, these record-holders really are extraordinary!

Name_____ Date_____

■ Answer the questions. Show your work.

1. How many fingers and toes do Menaria and Harne have **altogether**?

2. Harne is _____ years, _____ months, _____ days **older** than Menaria.

3. If polydactyly happens in 1 out of every 1,000 births, **estimate** how many cases would happen in 5,000 births. Explain your thinking.

4. What is the **average** length of the world's Longest Toenails?

5. **Estimate** the total length of all of McGrory's toes. Explain your thinking.

6. Use the answers from Questions 4 and 5 for the average length of each toenail and each toe length. **Estimate** how long each toe and toenail would be if the world's Longest Toenails were on the world's Longest Toes. Explain your thinking.

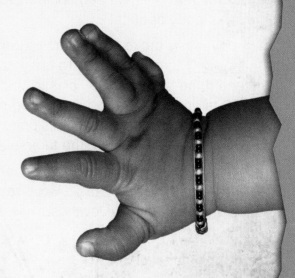

A REAL SPIDER MAN

■ Check this out!

Most Spiders on the Body for 30 Seconds

This is not your average spider record. Daniel Jovanoski (Macedonia) set a Guinness World Records™ record for having the Most Spiders on the Body for 30 Seconds. He had 200 spiders crawling on his body at once!

Jovanoski broke the record in Rome, Italy, on March 24, 2010. To break the record, he laid in a thick, plastic box. Then, 200 tarantulas were poured on top of him. Spiders crawled around on his body for 30 seconds. If that was not enough, the tarantulas left behind slimy deposits.

After 30 seconds, the spiders were wiped away from his body. He was the new record-holder! The previous record-holder had 150 spiders on his body. Now you know why Jovanoski has earned the title of spider man!

MORE AMAZING RECORDS

Longest Time of Full Body Contact with Ice: The record for Longest Time of Full Body Contact with Ice is 1 hour, 48 minutes, 21 seconds. The record was set by Chen Kecai of China on March 14, 2010.

Most Rhinestones on the Body: The record for Most Rhinestones on the Body is 33,139. The record was set on April 1, 2010, by Federica Ceracchi of Italy.

Name_____ Date_____

■ Answer the questions. Show your work.

1. Which record was broken most **recently**?

    A. Most Spiders on the Body for 30 Seconds (150)

    B. Most Spiders on the Body for 30 Seconds (200)

    C. Longest Time of Full Body Contact with Ice

    D. Most Rhinestones on the Body

2. Write an **equation** to show how many more spiders Jovanoski had on his body than the previous record-holder.

3. How many spiders would Jovanoski need to have on his body to beat the previous record by **twice** as much?

4. Kecai spent _____ seconds on the ice to break the record.

5. Ceracchi had **about** _____ times more rhinestones on her body than Jovanoski had spiders on his body.

6. How much more time would Kecai have had to stay on the ice for the record to have been an even 2 hours?

A TREASURE TROVE

■ Check this out!
Deepest Salvage of Cargo from a Shipwreck

This record-breaking group has taken treasure hunting to new depths by breaking the world record for bringing up the Deepest Salvage of Cargo from a Shipwreck. The cargo was brought up from 12,370 feet below the surface. Blue Water Recoveries (UK) brought up 394,627 pounds of copper and tin from the wreck. The group used an underwater robot named Grab 6000. The recovery took place in February 1997.

The sunken ship was a Dutch ship named SS *Alpherat*. It sank on December 21, 1943, during World War II. Blue Water Recoveries has found many famous shipwrecks that no one expected to find. The company has even broken 2 other Guinness World Records™ records for their recoveries!

MORE AMAZING RECORDS

Deepest Salvage: The greatest depth at which cargo has been successfully carried out is 17,251 feet. The wreck was a helicopter that crashed into the Pacific Ocean in August 1991. It was recovered in February 1992.

Deepest Salvage with Divers: The deepest recovery ever achieved with divers was on the wreck of the HMS *Edinburgh*. The ship had sunk on May 2, 1942, off northern Norway. It was recovered from 803 feet deep!

Name_____ Date_____

■ **Answer the questions. Show your work.**

1. Use **expanded notation** to write the number of pounds of copper and tin that were recovered from the SS *Alpherat*.

2. Draw a line to match each recovery to its depth in inches.

   Alpherat   207,012 inches

   helicopter   9,636 inches

   Edinburgh   148,440 inches

3. How long had the *Alpherat* been missing underwater?

4. How much longer had the *Alpherat* been underwater than the helicopter?

5. How much deeper was the recovery of the *Alpherat* than the recovery of the *Edinburgh*?

6. How much deeper was the recovery of the helicopter than the recovery of the *Edinburgh*? Explain your thinking.

A LARGE LADY OF LIBERTY

■ Check this out!

Heaviest Statue

The Statue of Liberty stands as a symbol of America's freedom. The Statue of Liberty is also the Heaviest Statue in the world. It weighs 27,156 tons!

The Statue of Liberty was a gift from France in 1885. It was shipped from France to the United States in 350 pieces.

The statue is made of 31 tons of copper, 125 tons of steel, and 27,000 tons of concrete. Lady Liberty stands 151 feet 1 inch from the base to the tip of the torch. Inside are 354 steps up to the crown. Her nose is 2 feet 6 inches long. The circumference of her waist is 35 feet. Her index finger is 8 feet long.

The statue stands on a pedestal that is 154 feet high, and the pedestal has 192 steps. This record-breaking statue deserves its place on a pedestal!

MORE AMAZING RECORDS

Largest Sheep Statue: The world's Largest Sheep Statue stands about 49 feet 2 inches tall. It is located in New South Wales, Australia.

Largest Single Piece Statue: The world's Largest Single Piece Statue stands 85 feet high. It is a carving made from 1 piece of white sandalwood. The statue is located in Beijing, China.

Name_____ Date_____

■ Answer the questions. Show your work.

1. Which of the following shows the weight of the Statue of Liberty in **expanded notation**?

   A. 200,000 + 7,000 + 1,000 + 50 + 6

   B. 20,000 + 7,000 + 100 + 50 + 6

   C. 27,000 + 100 + 50 + 6

   D. 20,000 + 7,000 + 100 + 56

2. How tall is the Statue of Liberty from the base of the pedestal to the tip of the torch?

3. The Largest Single Piece Statue is _____ feet _____ inches **taller** than the world's Largest Sheep Statue.

4. The Statue of Liberty is made of copper, steel, and concrete. Draw a line to match each material with its amount **in pounds**.

   copper   250,000

   steel   62,000

   concrete   54,000,000

5. Is the Statue of Liberty's nose to index finger **proportion** the same as your nose to index finger **proportion**? Explain your thinking.

6. On another sheet of paper, draw a picture to show the **relative height** of the 3 record-setting statues on page 98.

© Carson-Dellosa

SHARE THE POWER

■ Check this out!

Longest Underwater Power Cable

Power cables carry electricity from one place to another. Some cables even run under the ocean. The ABB group broke the Guinness World Records™ record for the world's Longest Underwater Power Cable. It is 358.84 miles long. It weighs about 75.6 pounds per yard.

The cable connects power in Norway to power in the Netherlands. The cable took more than 3 years to place. It was first used on September 11, 2008.

This cable allows Norway and the Netherlands to share power. The cable was made to work efficiently and help the environment. It carries energy from water and wind sources.

MORE AMAZING RECORDS

Most Electricity Made by Pedaling Underwater: The record for the Most Electricity Made by Pedaling Underwater is 2,502.2 watt hours. The record was set by Lloyd Matthew Godson (Australia). Godson spent 14 days in a small habitat on the ground of an aquarium.

Most Advanced Underwater Holographic Camera: The HOLOMAR underwater holographic camera can record 3-D images of objects as small as 100 microns. 100 microns is about the width of an average human hair!

Name_____ Date_____

■ Answer the questions. Show your work.

1. Place a dot on the **number line** to represent the length in miles of the world's Longest Underwater Power Cable.

358   359

2. On January 1, 2010, how long had the power cable been in use in **years**, **months**, and **days**?

3. If the ABB group placed an equal amount of cable each year, **about** how many miles of cable did they place each year?

4. On average, **about** how many watt hours did Godson pedal each day underwater?

5. What is the length of the world's Longest Underwater Power Cable in feet?
   A. 4,306.08 feet
   B. 22,736,102 feet
   C. 1,894,675.2 feet
   D. 18,946,752 feet

6. **About** how much does the record-breaking power cable weigh? Round the answer to the nearest tens place to estimate.

THIS WILL MAKE YOUR HEAD SPIN!

■ Check this out!

Most Basketballs Spun at the Same Time on a Frame

Can you spin a basketball on your finger? Michael Kettman (USA) broke the world record for the Most Basketballs Spun at the Same Time on a Frame. He spun 28 basketballs! He broke the record on May 25, 1999.

Kettman began spinning basketballs when he was 4 years old. In 1987 when he was 15, he set a goal of spinning the most basketballs. The record at the time was 8 balls. He practiced 6 to 8 hours every day for 21 days. He broke the record by spinning 10 balls. That record was broken a few years later.

In 1997, Kettman decided to regain the record. For his next attempt, he kept 20 balls spinning at the same time!

MORE AMAZING RECORDS

Most Tops Spun at the Same Time: The record for Most Tops Spun at the Same Time is 275 by 275 people. The record was broken in Romania on March 2, 2009.

Most Plates Spun at the Same Time: The record for Most Plates Spun at the Same Time is 108. Dave Spathaky (UK) broke the record while on a TV show in Thailand in November 1992.

Most Yo-Yos Spun at the Same Time: Ben McPhee (USA) was able to keep 16 yo-yos spinning at the same time. He spun 10 yo-yos on a hook, 2 on his ears, 2 with his mouth, and 2 with his hands. McPhee broke this record at the London Toy Fair on January 26, 2010.

■ Answer the questions. Show your work.

1. If each of the 275 people had spun 2 tops at the same time, how many tops would have broken the record?

2. If all of the records on page 102 were set at the same time, how many basketballs, tops, plates, and yo-yos would have been spinning **altogether**?

3. A standard basketball weighs 22 ounces. Kettman was spinning a total of

_____ pounds _____ ounces when he broke the current record.

4. On another sheet of paper, make a **time line** of Kettman's life starting at the year he was born and including dates from the passage on page 102.

5. If Kettman practiced an **average** number of hours for 21 days, how many hours did he practice to break his first record?

6. If the record-holder for the Most Plates Spun at the Same Time organized the plates in equal rows, how many different **combinations** of rows and plates in each row could he make?

AT A LOSS FOR WORDS?

■ Check this out!

Largest Word Search Puzzle

Do you like word search puzzles? A word search puzzle looks like a box of mixed-up letters. But as you look closer, words start to appear. You can find many workbooks that are filled with word search puzzles. But, this word search was not in a workbook. It broke the record for the world's Largest Word Search Puzzle. It has an area of 36.55 square feet and includes 3,200 words and 18,000 letters!

The word search was presented at a book fair in Rio de Janeiro, Brazil. The company that made this word search publishes crossword puzzles too. Copies of this giant word search puzzle are for sale. So if you ever find yourself at a loss for words, try looking in this puzzle!

MORE AMAZING RECORDS

Largest Jigsaw Puzzle: The world's Largest Jigsaw Puzzle measured 58,435.1 square feet. It had 21,600 pieces!

Largest Mechanical Puzzle: *Quest*, a three-dimensional puzzle, stands 57 inches tall and has a diameter of 52 1/2 inches. It weighs 506 pounds. The puzzle has 6 sides and 209 pieces.

Smallest Jigsaw Puzzle: The world's Smallest Jigsaw Puzzle with at least 1,000 pieces measures 7.17 inches by 10.12 inches.

■ Answer the questions. Show your work.

1. The world's Largest Word Search Puzzle has 18,000 letters. If every letter of the alphabet were in the puzzle an **equal number** of times, about how many of each letter would be included?

2. If the words in the world's Largest Word Search Puzzle averaged 5 letters each, **how many** total letters would have been included in the puzzle? (Do not count letters that are used in two words.)

3. Estimate the area of the Smallest Jigsaw Puzzle.

4. Write an equation to show how much larger the world's Largest Jigsaw Puzzle is than the world's Smallest Jigsaw Puzzle. Write your answer in **square inches**.

5. If each side of the Largest Mechanical Puzzle has the same number of pieces, **about** how many pieces are on each side?

6. Estimate the length of 1 of the sides of the world's Largest Word Search Puzzle. Explain your thinking.

JUMPING JACKS IN A FLASH

■ Check this out!

Most Jumping Jacks in 1 Minute

Doing jumping jacks is a great way to keep in shape. But, can you imagine doing 61 jumping jacks in 1 minute? That is exactly what Ashrita Furman (USA) did. Furman broke the record for the Most Jumping Jacks in 1 Minute. He did more than 1 jumping jack each second!

Furman set the record on May 17, 2008, in New York City. But, this was not the first record Furman set. In 1979, Furman broke his first world record by doing 27,000 jumping jacks!

Since then, Furman has broken a lot of records. He even holds the record for breaking the most Guinness World Records™ records—259 records since 1979! On April 14, 2009, Furman broke another world record. He became the first person to hold 100 records at the same time. Furman seems to like jumping from record to record as much as he likes jumping jacks!

MORE AMAZING RECORDS

Most Somersaults on a Trampoline in 1 Minute: Richard Cobbing (UK) set the world record for the Most Somersaults on a Trampoline in 1 Minute. He completed a total of 75 somersaults!

Most Cartwheels in 1 Minute: The world record for the Most Cartwheels in 1 Minute is 55. This record was set in 2009 by Marcio Barbosa of Brazil.

■ Answer the questions. Show your work.

1. Continuing at the same **rate**, how many jumping jacks would Furman do in 7 **minutes**?

2. Continuing at the same **rate**, how many cartwheels would Barbosa do in 1 **hour**?

3. Continuing at the same **rate**, how many somersaults would Cobbing do in 1 **day**?

4. If Furman continued at the same **rate**, **about** how long would it take him to complete 27,000 jumping jacks?

5. Which takes the **greatest amount** of time—a jumping jack, a somersault, or a cartwheel? Explain your thinking.

6. Using **estimation**, draw a line from each physical movement to the time it would take to do the movement 100 times.

100 jumping jacks	125 seconds
100 somersaults	101 seconds
100 cartwheels	92 seconds

GNARLY DUDE!

■ Check this out!

Longest Surfboard

Grab your board and get ready to shoot the tube! The world's Longest Surfboard is 39 feet 4 inches long and 9 feet 10 inches wide. It is 11.8 inches thick and weighs 1,763 pounds!

On March 5, 2005, a group of 47 surfers boarded the giant surfboard. Thousands of people came to watch. The event took place at Snapper Rocks in Queensland, Australia.

Nev Hyman (Australia) built the surfboard. He is famous for building surfboards for champion surfers. It took 1,102 pounds of foam and 79 gallons of resin to make the surfboard. He spent about 1 month building the board, and the cost was about $50,000.00!

Surfboards usually range from about 6 to 8 feet in length. They are between about 18 and 22 inches wide. They range between about 2.25 and 3.25 inches thick. As you can see, this is one gnarly board!

MORE AMAZING RECORDS

Longest Usable Golf Club: The world's Longest Usable Golf Club measures 13 feet 5 inches long. Karsten Maas of Denmark created and used the club. He hit a golf ball 403 feet 6 inches!

Longest Hockey Stick: The world's Longest Hockey Stick is 205 feet long. It weighs about 62,000 pounds. It is 40 times the size of a real hockey stick.

Longest Wooden Baseball Bat: The world's Longest Wooden Baseball Bat is 13 feet 5 inches long. Its circumference is 40 inches!

■ Answer the questions. Show your work.

1. Write the length of the world's Largest Surfboard as a **mixed number**.

2. The world's Longest Wooden Baseball Bat is about the same length as
   A. a size 13 shoe.
   B. 3 yardsticks end to end.
   C. a 10-story building.
   D. a ladder with 12 rungs.

3. An average golf club is about 40 inches long. **About** how many times longer is the world's Longest Usable Golf Club?

4. The golf ball hit by the world's Longest Usable Golf Club traveled _____ inches.

5. **Estimate** the **area** of the world's Largest Surfboard? Treat the surfboard as a rectangle.

6. **About** how long is an average hockey stick? Explain your thinking.

CHAIN REACTION

■ Check this out!

Most Dominoes Toppled in a Spiral

Have you ever watched the chain reaction of a line of dominoes? It is a lot of fun! Maximilian Poser (Germany) broke the world record for the Most Dominoes Toppled in a Spiral. A total of 28,800 dominoes fell with the push of just 1! Poser broke this record on April 14, 2009.

It took Poser 27 hours to set up the spiral. To be counted for the record, the topple must start with the push of a single domino. When the chain reaction stops, the fallen dominoes are counted. It does not matter how many dominoes were set up. The record is counted for the most dominoes toppled.

Many different domino records have been set. Poser also holds the record for the Most Dominoes Stacked on a Single Domino. He stacked 1,002 dominoes to break that record. The record for Most Dominoes Toppled by a Group is 4,345,027. That record was broken on November 14, 2008. Now, that is a chain reaction!

MORE AMAZING RECORDS

Most Dominoes Toppled by an Individual: The greatest number of dominoes set up and toppled by 1 person is 303,621. The record was set by Ma Li Hua (China) on August 18, 2003. Ma Li Hua worked an average of 10 hours each day from July 7 to August 17 to set up the dominoes.

Most Dominoes Toppled in 1 Minute: The record for Most Dominoes Toppled in 1 Minute is 53. Gail Buckley (UK) broke this record on March 20, 2010.

Name_____ Date_____

■ Answer the questions. Show your work.

1. How many **more** dominoes did the group topple than Poser's record for Most Dominoes Toppled in a Spiral?

2. On average, Poser set up more than _____ dominoes each hour to create his record-setting spiral.

3. A set of dominoes has 28 tiles. How many **sets** of dominoes did Poser use to create his record-setting spiral?

4. The time line below represents January 2003 through December 2010. Place the date of each domino event on the time line.

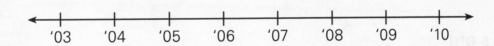

'03   '04   '05   '06   '07   '08   '09   '10

5. Using the **rate** of the Most Dominoes Toppled in 1 Minute, estimate how many minutes it took for Poser's dominoes to topple. Then, complete the table to solve the problem. Explain your thinking.

Minutes	Dominoes
1	53
10	
100	
1,000	

B-I-N-G-O!

■ Check this out!
Largest Game of Bingo

Do you enjoy the thrill of calling out "bingo"? Well, 70,080 people were hoping for that thrill. They played in the world's Largest Game of Bingo. This bingo game was played in Bogotá, Colombia. It was organized by a supermarket chain and took place on December 2, 2006. More than $250,000.00 was divided among the winners!

Bingo is a game of chance. Each player chooses 1 card with 24 numbers. The letters B, I, N, G, and O head the columns. Random numbers from 1 through 75 fill 5 rows, and 1 free space is in the center. Under the letter B can be any of the numbers 1 through 15. Under the letter I can be any of the numbers 16 through 30, and so on.

With 552,446,474,061,129,000,000,000,000 possible different cards, what are your chances of winning this game?

MORE AMAZING RECORDS

Largest Game of Simon Says: The world's Largest Game of Simon Says involved 12,215 people! The game took place at the Utah Summer Games opening ceremony in Cedar City, Utah, on June 14, 2007.

Largest Game of Hide-and-Seek: The world's Largest Game of Hide-and-Seek involved 188 people! The record was set by Kuniko Teramura and her friends (all Japan) on April 4, 2010. They played 3 rounds during the 1-hour game.

Longest Hopscotch Game: The world's Longest Hopscotch Game measures 15,762.93 feet. It was created by Victory Baptist Church and TOMS Shoes® in Tennessee as part of a fund-raising event. The event raised money to purchase shoes for the needy.

Name_____ Date_____

■ Answer the questions. Show your work.

1. How many **more** people played bingo than Simon Says?

2. Which of the following could **not** be a bingo number?
   - **A.** B7
   - **B.** I29
   - **C.** N52
   - **D.** O75

3. About how many minutes did each round of hide-and-seek take?

4. One mile equals 5,280 feet. The world's Longest Hopscotch Game was **almost**

   _____ miles long?

5. Show how many **combinations** of cards there would be if there were only B1, B2, and B3 in 1 column with rows.

6. Describe at least 10 different ways that 70,080 people could be organized **evenly** at tables.

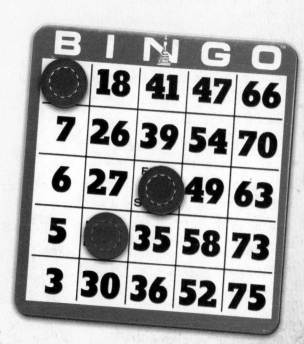

OUT OF GAS?

■ Check this out!
Heaviest Vehicle Pulled More Than 100 Feet by a Male

No, Kevin Fast (Canada) did not run out of gas. He set the Guinness World Records™ record for the world's Heaviest Vehicle Pulled More Than 100 Feet by a Male. The truck he pulled weighed 126,200 pounds!

Fast is not new to breaking records though. In fact, he held the previous record. His previous record was for pulling 125,660 pounds. He broke his record on a TV show on September 15, 2008. The show's costar even rode on the truck, adding an extra 92 pounds.

Fast likes to push himself. He likes to prove that when you put your mind (and muscle) to something, you can do it. He also broke a record by pulling an airplane. What do you think he will try to pull next?

MORE AMAZING RECORDS
Heaviest Aircraft Pulled by a Wheelchair Team: The record for Heaviest Aircraft Pulled by a Wheelchair Team is 143,675 pounds. The team of 38 wheelchair users pulled the aircraft about 328 feet!

Heaviest Vehicle Pulled by 1 Traction Kite: One 750-square-foot traction kite, which is shaped like a parachute, pulled a 55,115-pound boat at about 8 miles per hour for 45 minutes.

Name_____ Date_____

■ Answer the questions. Show your work.

1. Use **expanded notation** to write the weight of the truck that Fast pulled to break the current record.

2. Fast broke his own record by _____ pounds.

3. Which lists the 3 vehicles from page 114 from **lightest** to **heaviest**?
   A. aircraft, truck, boat
   B. boat, truck, aircraft
   C. boat, aircraft, truck
   D. truck, aircraft, boat

4. Based on the records on page 114, what was the **total** weight of the 3 vehicles pulled?

5. **About** how far did the traction kite pull the boat? Explain your thinking.

6. **Estimate** how much weight in pounds a team of 50 members in wheelchairs could pull. Explain your thinking.

GO TEAM!

■ Check this out!

Fastest Time to Visit All NFL Stadiums

Some football fans paint their faces with team colors. But, this football fan broke a world record! Peter Baroody (USA) broke the record for the Fastest Time to Visit All NFL Stadiums. He watched 32 complete National Football League (NFL) games at the 31 NFL stadiums in 107 days!

Baroody watched his first game on September 5, 2002, in New York. He watched his last game on December 22, 2002, in Kansas City. The 32 complete games of football took a total of about 99 hours. Baroody even broke this record without getting on an airplane. He drove a car to all 31 stadiums. He drove a total of 30,400 miles. Baroody is one record-setting football fan!

MORE AMAZING RECORDS

Fastest Time to Visit All Major League Baseball (MLB) Stadiums: The fastest time to visit and watch a complete game in every major league baseball park is 29 days. This record was set by Michael Wenz and Jacob Lindhorst (both USA). They saw the games between June 12 and July 10, 2005.

Fastest Time to Visit All English Football League (EFL) Stadiums: Ken Ferris (UK) watched a league match at all 92 league stadiums in England and Wales. It took him 237 days. He watched the games between September 10, 1994, and May 6, 1995.

Name_____ Date_____

■ Answer the questions. Show your work.

1. The amount of time it took Baroody to watch the games in all 31 NFL

   stadiums equals _____ weeks, _____ days.

2. A football game is **about** _____ hours long.

3. Which equation shows the average number of miles Baroody traveled each day?
   - **A.** 30,440 ÷ 107 = 284.5 miles
   - **B.** 30,440 ÷ 31 = 982 miles
   - **C.** 30,440 ÷ 17 = 1,790.5 miles
   - **D.** 30,440 ÷ 99 = 307.47 miles

4. Draw a line to match each record with the time it took to complete in months.

   visit to all NFL stadiums   about 1 month

   visit to all MLB stadiums   about 3 months

   visit to all EFL games   about 8 months

5. If Baroody traveled an average speed of 45 miles per hour, about how many **hours**
   did he drive during the 107 days?

6. For **about** how many hours did Baroody do something
   other than watch a football game or drive during the
   107 days? Explain your thinking.

AROUND THE WORLD

■ Check this out!

Longest Journey by Skateboard

Have you heard stories of people who travel around the world? Rob Thomson (New Zealand) took a journey in a unique way. He made the world's Longest Journey by Skateboard. He skateboarded 7,555 miles across 3 continents!

Thomson started his journey in Switzerland on June 24, 2007. He ended the European leg of his trip in London on August 4, 2007.

The North American leg of his trip started in Florida on December 7, 2007. Thomson traveled 3,435 miles across the United States. He ended the second leg in Los Angeles, California, on April 3, 2008.

MORE AMAZING RECORDS

Longest Journey Swimming: The record for the world's Longest Journey Swimming is 3,273.38 miles. It was set by Martin Strel (Slovenia). He swam the entire length of the Amazon River in 67 days.

Longest Journey Walking Backward: Plennie L. Wingo (USA) walked 8,000 miles backward! He walked across the United States from Santa Monica, California, to New York City. He then took a ship to Europe and ended his journey in Istanbul, Turkey. Wingo started his journey on April 15, 1931, and ended it on October 24, 1932.

Thomson started the final leg of his trip on the western side of China on April 27, 2008. He skateboarded 3,393 miles, mostly along the China National Highway. He ended his journey on September 28, 2008. On his journey, he wore out 3 pairs of shoes and 3 skateboards. Maybe it was 1 per continent?

Name_____ Date_____

■ **Answer the questions. Show your work.**

1. Use **<**, **>**, or **=** to make the statement true.

   the world's Longest Journey Swimming 3,273 $\frac{1}{2}$ miles

2. How many miles did Thomson skateboard through Europe?

3. Number the 3 journeys below from **shortest** length of time to **longest** length of time.

   _____ journey by skateboard   _____ journey swimming

   _____ journey walking backward

4. How many **more** miles did Thomson skateboard than Strel swam?

5. On average, **about** how many miles did Strel swim each day?

6. Create a **time line** showing the legs of Thomson's journey on skateboard.

HEY, BATTER BATTER!

■ Check this out!

Fastest Baseball Pitch by a Female

Next time you are up at bat, be glad Lauren Boden (USA) is not the pitcher. She set the Guinness World Records™ record for the world's Fastest Baseball Pitch by a Female. Her record pitch traveled 65 miles per hour!

Boden set this record on April 19, 2008, when she was only 15 years old. She also made history at her high school. She was the first girl to make the baseball team. She played for Lakeside High School in Atlanta, Georgia. Boden is 1 of a set of triplets. All 3 of the girls, plus a younger sister, play baseball.

In 2010, Boden graduated first in her class. Her 2 sisters shared second-place honors. They are stars both on the field and in the classroom.

MORE AMAZING RECORDS

Fastest Baseball Pitch by a Male: The record for the world's Fastest Baseball Pitch by a Male was 100.9 miles per hour! Professional baseball pitcher Nolan Ryan (USA) threw the record-setting pitch on August 20, 1974. Ryan played for the California Angels at the time.

Fastest Softball Pitch by a Female: The record for the world's Fastest Softball Pitch by a Female is 68.9 miles per hour. Zara Mee (Australia) threw this pitch on May 8, 2005.

Name_____ Date_____

■ Answer the questions. Show your work.

1. Round Nolan Ryan's pitch to the nearest whole number.

2. What is the **difference** between the speeds of the baseball thrown by Ryan and the baseball thrown by Boden?

3. How much faster did the fastest softball travel than Boden's baseball?

4. How old was Boden on April 19, 2010?

5. Which is **closest** to the speed of Boden's baseball pitch?
    A. a child skating
    B. a car traveling through a parking lot
    C. a car traveling on a highway
    D. a dog running in a park

6. Ryan was famous for pitching no-hitter games. A baseball game has 9 innings, and 3 outs are allowed in each inning. How many strikeouts would Ryan have to pitch to pitch 6 no-hitter games?

PING, PONG, AND REPEAT

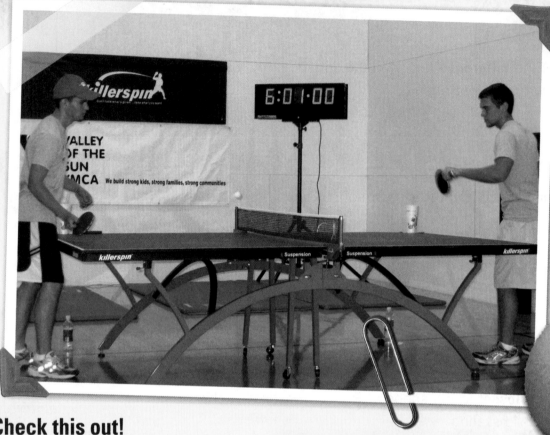

■ Check this out!

Longest Ping-Pong Rally

How long can you keep a ping-pong ball in play? Ask Brian and Steve Seibel (both USA). They had a ping-pong rally that lasted 8 hours, 15 minutes, 1 second. That is longer than the average full day of school! They played the game on August 14, 2004, in Phoenix, Arizona.

Ping-pong is another name for table tennis. Most ping-pong tables are 9 feet by 5 feet. A white line is painted down the middle from end to end.

A rally is the back-and-forth between players until a point is made. A ping-pong match lasts until someone scores 21 points. Imagine how long the match would be if each rally were this long!

MORE AMAZING RECORDS

Longest Tennis Rally: The world's Longest Tennis Rally lasted 15 hours, with 25,944 strokes between the players! Ettore Rossetti and Angelo A. Rossetti (both USA) set the record on August 9, 2008.

Longest Time Controlling a Tennis Ball Using Feet: In November 1999, Jacek Guzowski (Poland) kept a tennis ball in the air using only his feet for 5 hours, 28 minutes, 59 seconds. His feet touched the ball 35,000 times!

Longest Time Controlling a Ping-Pong Paddle and Ball: The record for Longest Time Controlling a Ping-Pong Paddle and Ball is 4 hours, 39 minutes, 52 seconds. It was set by Deepak Sharma Bajagain (Nepal) in December 2009.

Name_____ Date_____

■ Answer the questions. Show your work.

1. The **perimeter** of a ping-pong table is _____ feet.

2. If the record-setting ping-pong rally started at 10:00 A.M., what time did it end?

3. What time would the ping-pong rally have **started** if it finished at 7:00 P.M.?

4. Draw a line to match each record to its time in minutes. (Seconds are not counted.)

ping-pong rally	900 minutes
tennis rally	328 minutes
time controlling a tennis ball	495 minutes
time controlling a ping-pong paddle and ball	279 minutes

5. How much longer was the world's Longest Tennis Rally than the world's Longest Ping-Pong Rally?

6. About how many times did Guzowski touch the tennis ball **per minute**? Explain your thinking.

THE KARATE MASTER

■ Check this out!

Fastest Martial Arts Punch

Many people get a kick out of karate. But, this karate master got more than just a kick. Master John Ozuna (USA) set the Guinness World Records™ record for the world's Fastest Martial Arts Punch. Using high-speed photography, his punch was clocked at 43.3 miles per hour!

Master Ozuna broke the record on June 14, 2008, at his K.O. Kung Fu school in San Jose, California. Master Ozuna has been a martial arts teacher since 1981. He is a Master Black Belt in kung fu.

MORE AMAZING RECORDS

Highest Assisted Martial Arts Kick: The Highest Assisted Martial Arts Kick is 13 feet 11 inches. It was set by Brett Sawley (UK) on April 7, 2009. He had 2 assistants to help throw him toward the target.

Largest Martial Arts Display: The record for world's Largest Martial Arts Display included 33,996 people on August 8, 2009. The event was organized for the first national Fitness Day in China.

On the same day, Master Ozuna broke another world record. He broke the world record for the Most Punches in 1 Minute. The previous record was 702 punches. Master Ozuna beat the record by punching 713 times in 1 minute. That is almost 12 punches per second. Master Ozuna obviously gets a kick out of punching!

Name_____ Date_____

■ Answer the questions. Show your work.

1. Master Ozuna **beat** the previous record of Most Punches in 1 Minute by

   _____ punches.

2. If you **round** the world's Highest Assisted Martial Arts Kick to the nearest foot, the kick

   reached about _____ feet.

3. Write the miles per hour of the world's Fastest Martial Arts Punch in **words**.

4. For how many years had Master Ozuna been teaching martial arts when he broke
   the records?

5. If Master Ozuna continued punching at the same **rate** as
   his record-breaking punches, how many times would he
   punch in 5 minutes?

6. Could the number of people in the world's Largest Martial
   Arts Display be divided into 2 equal groups? 3 equal groups?
   6 equal groups? Explain your thinking.

ANSWER KEY

Page 11

1. 1964; 2. 16 inches; 3. 100,000 colors; 10,000 x 10 = 100,000; 4. dogs; 5. B; 6. Answer should include a 2-column table that lists the names of the animals and shows their number of receptors: mantis shrimp–8, humans–3, dogs–2. Title could be "Animal Eye Color Receptors."

Page 13

1. 1 insect, 2 rabbit, 3 lizard; 2. 3 1/4 feet; 3. 2 feet 6 inches or 30 inches; 4. 56.1 inches; 5. A; 6. More than 5 times as large; 4 times Alice's length is about 160 inches; 5 times Alice's length is about 200 inches; 187 is more than 5 times and less than 6 times.

Page 15

1. 8; 2. 2.9 inches; 3. 4; 4. About 1,500 times; 5. C; 6. About 140–144 times

Page 17

1. 50; 2. Almost 14 strides; 3. Students should mark points at 34 (monkey), 35 (pronghorn), and 36.8 (Nyana); 4. Lines should be drawn between 3,936 inches and 6.19 seconds; 327 yards and about 18 seconds; 1,640 feet and about 30 seconds; and 164 feet and about 3 seconds; 5. 812 strides; 6. About 4,000 strides; he would travel about 18 miles in 1/2 hour, and there are about 95,000 feet in 18 miles; 95,000 ÷ 24 is about 4,000.

Page 19

1. B; 2. Lines should be drawn between 90° and 1/4 of a roll; 180° and 1/2 of a roll; 270° and 3/4 of a roll; 3. 1/18; 4. 14.61 inches per second; 5. About 2 times faster; 6.

1 sec.	15
10 sec.	150
30 sec.	450
1 min.	900

Rule: 15 x s

Page 21

1. B; 2. 5 years; 3. butterfly (2,880), caribou (2,982), whale (5,095), tuna (5,800), tern (10,875); 4. 2; 5. 120 pounds. Divide 1,200 pounds by 10. 6. About 16 days; 5,800 divided by 15 equals about 387. Divide 387 by 24 (hours in a day) to get about 16 days.

Page 23

1. 3 hands; 2. 18.75 inches; 3. B; 4. Yes; 82.75 inches > 80 inches; 5. 57 hands; 6. 3 horse, 1 mule, 4 giraffe, 2 ox. Drawing should show the mule only slightly shorter than the ox. The horse should be slightly taller than the ox. The giraffe should be more than twice as tall as the mule, horse, and ox.

Page 25

1. A; 2. B; 3. 0.15; 4. $437,000; 5. $15,201,000; 6. about 1/3 inch

Page 27

1. 79.45 inches; 2. 114 inches or 9 feet 6 inches; 3. 4 7/12 feet; 4. about 1 1/2 times; 5. 1 foot 4 inches

Page 29

1. 31 years; 2. D; 3. 0.8 inch; 4. Archie, because he finishes a 13-inch course in 2 minutes, and it takes Verne more than 2 minutes to complete a course shorter than 13 inches; 5. The line should be marked 16 inches long, with hash marks at about 2 1/2 inches from each end; end sections labeled 2 1/2 inches and center section labeled 11 inches. The rounded length of the snail is 16 inches. The rounded length of the shell is 11 inches. That leaves 5 inches or 2 1/2 inches at the front and back; 6. About 3 ounces; the giant snail weighs about 2 ounces per inch. Using that measurement to estimate, the garden snail would weigh about 3 ounces.

Page 31

1. A; 2. 3 feet 4 inches; 3. 12,000 feet; 4. 77.5 inches or 6 feet 5.5 inches; 5. B; 6. Answers will vary but will be around 3 to 4 inches.

Page 33

1. 15 years old; 2. B; 3. 973,981 more dogs; 4. Snag recovered seven hundred forty-seven million dollars more than Trepp. 5. 11 1/2 inches; 6. Drawing should show a dog 11/16 of an inch tall and 1 inch long with the tail 7/16 inches long.

Page 35

1. 5; 2. Less. Twice the scorpion's length could be up to 14 inches. 3. C; 4. 432 ounces; 5. 6 •————— 7; 6. Answers will vary. If you average 12, 15, and 34 pounds, the result will not be a typical weight. The 34 pounds will distort the results. The more typical samples you add to the data, the less the outlier will skew the results.

Page 37

1. C; 2. 16 feet 8 inches; 3. About 43 days; 4. Lines should be drawn between yucca and 300 inches; bamboo and 1,050 inches; kelp and 399 inches; tree and 33 inches; 5. 130 x 12 = x; x = 1,560 inches; 6. About 9 days; 13.3 inches is a little more than 1 foot a day, so in 10 days, it will have grown more than 10 feet; in 9 days, it will have grown about 10 feet.

Page 39

1. 17.25; 2. D; 3. 767; 4. About 2,300,000 square feet; 5. About 760,000 square feet. Carlsbad Caverns is 3 times smaller than 2,300,000 square feet. 6. Measure 25 feet 92 times.

Page 41

1. D; 2. Multiply the weight in pounds by 16. (16 ounces in a pound); 3. Lines should be drawn between watermelon and 4,300.8 ounces; mango and 121.12 ounces; cauliflower and 867 ounces; carrot and 301 ounces; tomato and 124 ounces; 4. About 35 mangoes; 35 mangoes would weigh 264.95 pounds. Answers should explain something about finding the number of times 7 will go into 268. Answers more than 30 and fewer than 40 should be accepted. 5. d = 19.5 / 3.14; 6. Slice off the top of the carrot and measure from edge to edge across the middle point.

Page 43

1. A football field is 300 feet. Dunes can be 90 feet higher. 2. Three million five hundred thousand square miles; 3. A; 4. The United States is larger by 37,441 square miles; 5. 44 + 56 = 100 degrees; 6. 188; Students should draw a number line with –90, 0, and 98 marked and a span across the top from –90 to 98 labeled 188.

Page 45

1. B; 2. About 14 tons; 3. 48 inches; 4. A; 5. About 70; 6. One arrow is about the same length as 5 football fields. 300 feet are in 1 football field, so 5 x 300 = 1,500, which is close to 1,600.

Page 47

1. less than; 2. 45; 3.10 years, 7 months, 28 days; 4. C; 5. About 6; 6. About 1/12 or 0.08 of a mile per second; 300 miles per hour ÷ 60 minutes = 5 miles per minute; divide by 60 seconds to get 5/60.

Page 49

1. C; 2. 3,144 inches; 3. 2; 4. No. The Weddell Sea is the clearest water, and it only registered to a depth of 262 feet. The bottom of Dean's Blue Hole is 663 feet. 5. About 800,000 feet long; 6. About 25 miles wide; Divide the rounded area by the rounded length: 5,000 ÷ 200.

Page 51

1. About 2,000 trees; 2. 10 hours, 45 minutes; 3. 1 Most Trees Planted by a Team in 24 Hours; 3 Most Trees Planted in a Public Park; 4 Most Palm Trees Planted in 10 Years; 2 Most Trees Planted at the Same Time; 4. 48,549,144 trees; 5. About 7,000 trees per acre; 6. The 300 people in 24 hours: They each planted about 2,000 trees, while the 169,920 people each planted about 35 trees.

Page 53

1. 640; 2. greater than; 3. B; 4. 3,250 times larger; 5. About 12,000 square inches; 6. Students should divide the time line at the following points: 1998 moon meteorite, 1962 Martian meteorite, 1920 largest meteorite; students should mark 42 years between the first 2 dates and 36 years between the second 2 dates.

Page 55

1. 28 feet; 2. 1,110 toes; 3. C; 4. 3; 5. Unlikely. Rogue waves are not usual. 6. 12%; 112 − 100 = 12; 12 is 12 percent of 100.

Page 57

1. Thirteen thousand two hundred four dollars; 2. C; 3. 25,173 pounds more; 4. About 3 inches; 5. 13,888 people; 868 pounds x 16 ounces; 6. 61 feet 4 inches long; each slice would have a length equal to the radius or 1/2 the diameter of the pizza.

Page 59

1. 1,726 people; 2. 12,583 more people; 3. 1 Largest Human National Flag; 3 Largest Human Logo; 2 Largest Human Rainbow; 4. 3 years, 5 days; 5. 65,178 people; 6. Accept any reasonable answer. Possible answer: about 100 rows with 217 or 218 people

Page 61

1. 2 per second; 2. almonds, corn, potatoes, eggs; 3. 16 years, 9 months, 28 days; 4. 45 seconds; 5. About 15 seconds; 17 ÷ 4 is about 4 ears per person per minute; 60 seconds ÷ 4 = 15 seconds; 6. Between 4 and 5 pounds in a minute

Page 63

1. B; 2. 5 years, 5 months, 1 day; 3. 60 quarts; 4. About 7 to 8 seconds; 5. About 90–100 minutes (24 people in 3 minutes = 8 people in 1 minute; 8 × 90 = 720; 8 × 100 = 800); 6. About 30 ounces

Page 65

1. $775,000 more; 2. 640 fewer people; 3. B; 4. 1,624 people; 5. 26 miles; twice as long as a half marathon; 2 x 13 = 26; 6. 58

Page 67

1. 4 Hotel Everest View; 3 kite; 1 aircraft; 2 car; 2. Less than 3 miles. 5,280 feet are in 1 mile. 3 miles would be more than 15,000 feet. 3. Answers will vary. The wingspan should be a little less than twice the height. 4. 25,700-foot-long rope; 5. About 8 or 9 times higher; 6. About 500 feet per second

Page 69

1. 5.91 seconds; 2. 35 seconds; 3. 7.81 seconds; 4. Text in Arabic. 43.44 seconds is less than 45.09 seconds. 5. About 25 seconds per country; 148 seconds ÷ 6 countries; 6. About 4 characters per second; the message is 160 characters; 160 ÷ about 40 seconds

Page 71

1. $712; 2. $14; 3. $50; 4. $35.60; 5. About $1,250 per cherry; 6. More than $1,500, because the bill without taxes and tip comes to $1,488. The tip alone should be about $300, even before taxes.

Page 73

1. D; 2. 665,000 more dahlias; 3. 1,130; 4. Carpet by 61,047 square feet; 5. 2,073.28 feet; 6. About 100 carnations; about 100,000 carnations ÷ about 1,000 inches

Page 75

1. 37.339 acres; 2. A; 3. 632,979.32 square feet smaller; 4. About 1,600,000 square feet; 5. The tree maze path is about 4,000 feet longer. The hedge maze is 13,000 feet long, and the tree maze is about 17,000 feet long. 6. About 64,000 boxes

Page 77

1. A; 2. 10,000,000 + 5,000,000 + 200,000; 3. $331,461; 4. $1,268,539; 5. About 10 cents each; 6. About 150 escudos = $1 U.S.; about 45,000,000 escudos = about $300,000; cancel zeros then 450 ÷ 3 = 150

Page 79

1. 13 miles; 2. B; 3. Four thousand six hundred sixty miles; 4. 3 months, 18 days; 5. 295 seconds; 6. A little more than 7 days; 650 x 7 = 4,550 miles, so a little more would be about 4,660 miles.

Page 81

1. 49 feet; 2. 75,360,000 cubic feet; 3. 150,000; 4. 823 feet; 5. Answers will vary. It should be concluded that it must be less than 550 feet high because it is a lot longer than the Grand Coulee Dam, which is the world's Largest Concrete Dam. 6. Answers will vary but should show the Grande Dixence about 1/2 as long as the Grand Coulee, and the Kiev Dam about 30 times as long as the Grand Coulee.

Page 83

1. C; 2. 49 miles per hour; 0.71 is closer to 1 more than 0 more; 3. 39 days; 4. 7,414 miles more; 5. About 235 miles; 6. About 190 hours; about 9,500 miles ÷ about 50 miles per hour

Page 85

1. B; 2. 93 feet 2 inches; 3. 22 years old; 4. 59 feet; 5. C; 6. About 2 times, which is not very far relative to its size. It is like a 6-inch-wide paper airplane going 1 foot, which is not very far.

Page 87

1. C; 2. About 4 pounds each; 3. 157.86 more pounds; 4. 3; 5. 573 ———•— 574; 6. Answers will vary. Possible answer may be that each person weighs 150 pounds, and the pot weighs 273.86 pounds.

Page 89

1. 277.5; 2. A; 3. 23 more years; 4. 1/10 of an inch

Week	Inches
1	0.02
2	0.04
3	0.06
4	0.08
5	0.10

5. 50 weeks; 6. The total measurement would be less. 0.9 total is left out, and 0.4 is added, so the difference would be 0.5 less.

Page 91

1. False; 2. 6; 3. 325 blocks high

Minutes	Bricks
1	65
2	130
3	195
4	260
5	325

4. About 15 cans high; 5. 2,883 chrysanthemums; 6. About 15 minutes

Page 93

1. 24 fingers + 26 toes = 50; 2. 10 years, 7 months, 1 day; 3. 5 cases; 4. 8.7 inches; 5. Answers will vary but should have the toes between 1.5 and 5 inches long. The total will be more than 22 inches and less than 43 inches. 6. Answers will vary. Reasonable answers will add 8.7 inches to the length of each toe.

Page 95

1. D; 2. 200 – 150 = 50; 3. 300 spiders; 4. 6,501; 5. 150; 6. 11 minutes, 39 seconds

Page 97

1. 300,000 + 90,000 + 4,000 + 600 + 20 + 7; 2. Lines should be drawn between *Alpherat* and 148,440; helicopter and 207,012; *Edinburgh* and 9,636; 3. 53 years, 2 months; 4. 52 years, 8 months; 5. 11,567 feet deeper; 6. 16,448 feet deeper. Answers will vary but may suggest that the depth of the ocean is different off the coast versus in the middle of the ocean.

Page 99

1. B; 2. 305 feet 1 inch; 3. 35 feet 10 inches; 4. Lines should be drawn between copper and 62,000; steel and 250,000; concrete and 54,000,000; 5. No. The index finger on a human is only about twice as long as the nose. On the Statue of Liberty, it is about 3 times as long; 6. Answers will vary but should show the Statue of Liberty almost twice the size of the statue made from a single piece and 3 times the height of the sheep statue.

Page 101

1. 358 ———•359; 2. 1 year, 3 months, 20 days; 3. About 120 miles each year; 4. About 178 watt hours; 5. C; 6. About 50,400,000 pounds; multiply miles by 5,280 to calculate about 1,895,000 feet; divide feet by 3 to calculate about 630,000 yards; multiply by 80 to find the pounds.

Page 103

1. 550 tops; 2. 427 total; 3. 38 pounds 8 ounces; 4. Time line may include: 1972, born; 1976 started spinning basketballs; 1987 broke first record spinning 10 balls; 1997 broke record spinning 20 balls; 1999 broke record spinning 28 balls. 5. 147 hours; 6. 12 combinations: 1 row of 108; 2 rows of 54; 3 rows of 36; 4 rows of 27; 6 rows of 18; 9 rows of 12; 12 rows of 9; 18 rows of 6; 27 rows of 4; 36 rows of 3; 54 rows of 2; 108 rows of 1

Page 105

1. 692 times; 2. 16,000 letters; 3. About 70 square inches; 4. (58,435.1 × 12) – (7.17 × 10.12) = 701,148.64 square inches; 5. About 35 pieces on each side; 6. Accept any reasonable answer. 6 feet is the most likely estimate. If the puzzle is a square, each side would be 6 feet for the area to be 36 square feet.

Page 107

1. 427 jumping jacks; 2. 3,300 cartwheels; 3. 108,000 somersaults; 4. about 450 hours; 5. cartwheel; the least number of these can be done in 1 minute; 6. Lines should be drawn between jumping jacks and 101 seconds; somersaults and 92 seconds; cartwheels and 125 seconds

Page 109

1. 39 1/3 inches; 2. D; 3. About 4 times; 4. 4,842; 5. About 390 square feet; 6. About 5 feet long. The information says 205 is 40 times the size of an average hockey stick.

Page 111

1. 4,316,227 more dominoes; 2. 1,000; 3. 1,029 sets; 4. Time line may include: Aug. 18, 2003, Nov. 14, 2008, April 14, 2009, and March 20, 2010; 5. About 500 minutes. 28,800 is about half of 53,000.

Minutes	Dominoes
1	53
10	530
100	5,300
1,000	53,000

Page 113

1. 57,865 more people; 2. C; 3. About 20 minutes; 4. 3; 5. There are 6 possible combinations: B1 B2 B3; B1 B3 B2; B2 B1 B3; B2 B3 B1; B3 B1 B2; B3 B2 B1; 6. Accept any reasonable answer. Possible answers include: 5 tables of 14,016 people; 6 tables of 11,680 people; 8 tables of 8,760 people; 10 tables of 7,008 people; 12 tables of 5,840 people; 15 tables of 4,672 people; 20 tables of 3,504 people; 24 tables of 2,920 people; 7,008 tables of 10 people; 8,760 tables of 8 people; 11,680 tables of 6 people; 14,016 tables of 5 people.

Page 115

1. 100,000 + 20,000 + 6,000 + 200; 2. 540; 3. B; 4. 324,990 total pounds; 5. 6 miles. 3/4 of 8 miles per hour because it pulled for 45 minutes. 6. About 180,000 pounds; About 40 members pulled about 144,000 pounds, so 10 people would pull about 1/4 of that, or 36,000 pounds; So, 50 members would pull 144,000 + 36,000 pounds.

Page 117

1. 15 weeks, 2 days; 2. 3; 3. A; 4. Lines should be drawn between NFL games and about 3 months; MLB games and about 1 month; EFL games and about 8 months; 5. About 675 hours of driving; 6. 1,794 hours; 2568 hours in 107 days minus 99 hours of football minus 675 hours of driving

Page 119

1. <; 2. 727 miles; 3. 2 journey on a skateboard; 1 journey swimming; 3 journey walking backward; 4. 4,281.62 miles; 5. About 50 miles per day; 6. Time line should include June 2007 started journey; August 2007 finished European leg; December 2007 started North American leg; April 2008 finished North American leg; April 2008 started in China; September 2008 journey ended.

Page 121

1. 101 miles per hour; 2. 35.9 miles per hour; 3. 3.9 miles per hour; 4. 17 years old; 5. C; 6. 162 strikeouts

Page 123

1. 28; 2. 6:15 P.M.; 3. 10:45 A.M.; 4. Lines should be drawn between ping-pong rally and 495 minutes; tennis rally and 900 minutes; time controlling a tennis ball and 328 minutes; time controlling a ping-pong paddle and ball and 279 minutes; 5. 6 hours, 44 minutes, 59 seconds; 6. About 100 times per minute; he touched the ball 35,000 times in about 350 minutes.

Page 125

1. 11; 2. 14; 3. Forty-three and three tenths; 4. 27 years; 5. 3,565 punches; 6. Yes, it is an even number; yes, it is divisible by 3; yes, it is divisible by 6.